AFRO-AMERICAN
FOLKSONGS

AFRO-AMERICAN FOLKSONGS

A Study
in Racial and National Music

HENRY EDWARD KREHBIEL

FREDERICK UNGAR PUBLISHING CO.
NEW YORK

TO MY FRIEND
HORATIO W. PARKER, Mus. Doc.
PROFESSOR OF MUSIC AT YALE UNIVERSITY

Republished 1962

Third Printing, 1971

Printed in the United States of America

ISBN 0-8044-5571-6

Library of Congress Catalog Card No. 62-10896

PREFACE

This book was written with the purpose of bringing a species of folksong into the field of scientific observation and presenting it as fit material for artistic treatment. It is a continuation of a branch of musical study for which the foundation was laid more than a decade ago in a series of essays with bibliographical addenda printed in the New York "Tribune," of which journal the author has been the musical reviewer for more than thirty years. The general subject of those articles was folksongs and their relation to national schools of composition. It had come to the writer's knowledge that the articles had been clipped from the newspaper, placed in envelopes and indexed in several public libraries, and many requests came to him from librarians and students that they be republished in book-form. This advice could not be acted upon because the articles were mere outlines, ground-plans, suggestions and guides to the larger work or works which the author hoped would the be the result of his instigation.

Folksong literature has grown considerably since then, especially in Europe, but the subject of paramount interest to the people of the United States has practically been ignored. The songs created by the negroes while they were slaves on the plantations of the South have cried out in vain for scientific study, though "ragtime" tunes, which are their debased offspring, have seized upon the fancy of the civilized world. This popularity may be deplorable, but it serves at least to prove that a marvellous potency lies in the characteristic rhythmical element of the slave songs. Would not a wider and truer knowledge of their other characteristics as well lead to the creation of a better art than that which tickles the ears and stimulates the feet of the pleasure-seekers of London, Paris, Berlin and Vienna even more than it does those of New York?

The charm of the Afro-American songs has been widely recognized, but no musical savant has yet come to analyze them. Their two most obvious elements only have been copied by composers and dance-makers, who have wished to imitate them. These elements are the rhythmical propulsion which comes from the initial syncopation common to the bulk of them (the "snap" or "catch" which in an exaggerated form lies at the basis of "ragtime") and the frequent use of the five-tone or pentatonic scale. But there is much more that is characteristic in this body of melody, and this "more" has been neglected because it has not been uncovered to the artistic world. There has been no study of it outside of the author's introduction to the subject printed years ago and a few comments, called forth by transient phenomena, in the "Tribune" newspaper in the course of the last generation. This does not mean that the world has kept silent on the subject. On the contrary, there has been anything but a dearth of newspaper and platform talk about songs which the negroes sang in America when they were slaves, but most of it has revolved around the questions whether or not the songs were original creations of these native blacks, whether or not they were entitled to be called American and whether or not they were worthy of consideration as foundation elements for a school of American composition.

The greater part of what has been written was the result of an agitation which followed Dr. Antonin Dvořák's efforts to direct the attention of American composers to the beauty and efficiency of the material which these melodies contained for treatment in the higher artistic forms. Dr. Dvořák's method was eminently practical; he composed a symphony, string quartet and string quintet in which he utilized characteristic elements which he had discovered in the songs of the negroes which had come to his notice while he was a resident of New York. To the symphony he gave a title—"From the New World"—which measurably disclosed his purpose; concerning the source of his inspiration for the chamber compositions he said nothing, leaving it to be discovered, as it easily was, from the spirit, or feeling, of the music and the character of its melodic and rhythmic idioms. The eminent composer's aims, as well as his deed, were widely misunderstood at the time, and, for that matter, still are. They called out a clamor from one class of critics which disclosed nothing so much as their want of intelligent discrimination unless it was their ungenerous and illiberal attitude toward a body of American citizens to whom at the least must be credited the creation of a species of song in which an undeniably great composer had recognized artistic potentialities thitherto neglected, if not unsuspected, in the land of its origin. While the critics quarrelled, however, a group of American musicians acted on Dr. Dvořák's suggestion, and music in the serious, artistic forms, racy of the soil from which the slave songs had sprung, was produced by George W. Chadwick, Henry Schoenberg, Edward R. Kroeger and others.

It was thus that the question of a possible folksong basis for a school of composition which the world would recognize as distinctive, even national, was brought upon the carpet. With that question I am not concerned now. My immediate concern is to outline the course and method to be pursued in the investigations which I have undertaken. Primarily, the study will be directed to the music of the songs and an attempt be made by comparative analysis to discover the distinctive idioms of that music, trace their origins and discuss their correspondences with characteristic elements of other folk-melodies, and also their differences.

The burden is to be laid upon the music. The poetry of the songs has been discussed amply and well, never so amply or so well as when they were first brought to the attention of the world by a group of enthusiastic laborers in the cause of the freedmen during the War of the Rebellion. Though foreign travellers had written enthusiastically about the singing of the slaves on the Southern plantations long before, and though the so-called negro minstrels had provided an admired form of entertainment based on the songs and dances of the blacks which won unexampled popularity far beyond the confines of the United States, the descriptions were vague and general, the sophistication so great, that it may be said that really nothing was done to make the specific beauties of the unique songs of the plantations known until Miss McKim wrote a letter about them to Dwight's "Journal of Music," which was printed under the date of November 8, 1862.

In August, 1863, H. G. Spaulding contributed some songs to "The Continental Monthly," together with an interesting account of how they were sung and the influence which they exerted upon the singers. In "The Atlantic Monthly" for June, 1867, Colonel Thomas Wentworth Higginson printed the texts of a large number of songs and accompanied them with so sympathetic and yet keen an analysis of their psychology and structure that he left practically nothing for his successors to say on the subject. Booker T. Washington and W. E. Burghardt DuBois have only been able to echo him in strains of higher rhapsody. Much use was made of these articles by William Francis Allen in the preface of the first collection of the songs, entitled "Slave Songs of the United States," published by A. Simpson & Co. in New York in 1867. The observations of these writers and a few others make up practically the entire sum of what it is essential to know about the social, literary and psychological side of the folksongs of the American negroes. None of these early collectors had more than a smattering of musical knowledge, and none of them attempted to subject the melodies of the songs to analytical study.

Outside of the cursory and fragmentary notices of "The Tribune's" music reviewer called out by a few performances of the songs and the appearance of the collections which followed a popularization of the songs by the singing of the Jubilee Singers of the Fisk University and other choirs from the schools established for the higher education of the emancipated blacks, nothing of even a quasi-scientific character touching the melodies appeared during the last generation until M. Julien Tiersot, the distinguished librarian of the Paris Conservatory, published a monograph[1] (first in the Journal of the International Music Society, afterward separately) giving the results of his investigations into the folkmusic of Canada and the United States made during a

---

[1] "La Musique chez les Peuples indigènes de l'Amérique du Nord—États-Unis et Canada." Paris, Librairie Fischbacher; Leipsic and New York, Breitkopf & Härtel.

visit to America in the winter and spring of 1905-1906.
A few months ago a book entitled "Musik, Tanz und
Dichtung bei den Kreolen Amerikas," by Albert Friedenthal, was published in Berlin. M.Tiersot concerned himself chiefly with the Indians, though he made some keen
observations on the music of the black Creoles of Louisiana, and glanced also at the slave songs, for which he
formed a sincere admiration; the German folklorist treated
of negro music only as he found it influencing the dances
of the people of Mexico, Central America, South America
and the West Indies.

The writer of this book, therefore, had to do the work of
a pioneer, and as such will be satisfied if he shall succeed in
making a clearing in which successors abler than he shall
work hereafter.

The scope of my inquiry and the method which I have
pursued may be set forth as follows:

1. First of all it shall be determined what are folksongs, and whether
or not the songs in question conform to a scientific definition in respect of
their origin, their melodic and rhythmical characteristics and their psychology.

2. The question, "Are they American?" shall be answered.

3. Their intervallic, rhythmical and structural elements will be inquired
into and an effort be made to show that, while their combination into songs
took place in this country, the essential elements came from Africa; in other
words, that, while some of the material is foreign, the product is native; and,
if native, then American.

4. An effort will be made to disprove the theory which has been frequently
advanced that the songs are not original creations of the slaves, but only the
fruit of the negro's innate faculty for imitation. It will be shown that some
of the melodies have peculiarities of scale and structure which could not
possibly have been copied from the music which the blacks were privileged
to hear on the plantations or anywhere else during the period of slavery.
Correspondence will be disclosed, however, between these peculiarities and
elements observed by travellers in African countries.

5. This will necessitate an excursion into the field of primitive African
music and also into the philosophy underlying the conservation of savage
music. Does it follow that, because the American negroes have forgotten
the language of their savage ancestors, they have also forgotten all of their
music? May relics of that music not remain in a subconscious memory?

6. The influences of the music of the dominant peoples with whom the
slaves were brought into contact upon the rude art of the latter will have to
be looked into and also the reciprocal effect upon each other; and thus the
character and nature of the hybrid art found in the Creole songs and dances
of Louisiana will be disclosed.

To make the exposition and arrangement plain, I shall
illustrate them by musical examples. African music will

be brought forward to show the sources of idioms which have come over into the folksongs created by negroes in America; and the effect of these idioms will be demonstrated by specimens of song collected in the former slave States, the Bahamas and Martinique. Though for scientific reasons I should have preferred to present the melodies of these songs without embellishment of any sort, I have yielded to a desire to make their peculiar beauty and usefulness known to a wide circle of amateurs, and presented them in arrangements suitable for performance under artistic conditions.

For these arrangements I am deeply beholden to Henry T. Burleigh, Arthur Mees, Henry Holden Huss and John A. Van Broekhoven. An obligation of gratitude is also acknowledged to Mr. Ogden Mills Reid, Editor of "The New York Tribune," for his consent to the reprinting of the essays; to Mr. George W. Cable and The Century Company for permission to use some of the material in two of the former's essays on Creole Songs and Dances published in 1886 in "The Century Magazine;" and to Professor Charles L. Edwards, the American Folk-Lore Society, Miss Emily Hallowell and Harper & Brothers for like privileges.

H. E. KREHBIEL.

Blue Hill, Me.
Summer of 1913.

CONTENTS

[xi]

CONTENTS—*Continued*

CHAPTER I

FOLKSONGS IN GENERAL

———

The Characteristics of Folksongs—Folksongs De-
fined—Creative Influences—Folksong and
Suffering—Modes, Rhythms and Scales—
Russian and Finnish Music—Persistency
of Type—Music and Racial Ties—
Britons and Bretons

———

The purpose of this book is to study the origin and nature
of what its title calls Afro-American Folksongs. To fore-
fend, as far as it is possible to do so, against misconceptions
it will be well to have an understanding at the outset as
to terms and aims. It is essential, not only to an understanding of the argument but also to a necessary limitation
of the scope of the investigation, that the term "folksong"
be defined. The definition must not include too much
lest, at the last, it prove too compass to little. So as far as
possible the method of presentation must be rational and
scientific rather than rhetorical and sentimental, and the
argument be directed straight and unswervingly toward
the establishment of facts concerning a single and distinct
body of song, regardless of any other body even though the
latter be closely related or actually derived from the former.

It is very essential that the word folksong be understood
as having as distinctive a meaning as "folklore," "myth,"
"legend" or "*Märchen*"—which last word, for the sake of
accuracy, English folklorists have been forced to borrow
from the Germans. It will also be necessary in this exposition to appeal to the Germans to enforce a distinction
which is ignored or set aside by the majority of English
writers on folksong—popular writers, that is. The Germans
who write accurately on the subject call what I would
have understood to be folksong *das Volkslied;* for a larger
body of song, which has community of characteristics with
the folksong but is not of it, they have the term *volksthüm-*

liches Lied. This body of song embraces all vocal compositions which have come to be so fondly liked, loved, admired by the people that they have become a native and naïve popular utterance. So generous, indeed, is the term that it embraces not only the simple songs based on genuine folksong texts which musicians have set to music, and the large number of artistic compositions which imitate the sentiment and structure of folksongs, but also many lyrics made with conscious art by eminent composers. In the family circles of Germany and at popular gatherings one may hear not only Silcher's setting of "Zu Strassburg auf der Schanz" (which is music set by an artist to a folkpoem), but the same composer's melody to "Ich weiss nicht, was soll es bedeuten" (an artificial folkpoem by Heine), Weber's "Wir winden dir den Jungfernkranz" and Schubert's "Am Brunnen vor dem Thore" (which are artistic products in conception and execution). The English term "popular song" might well and properly be used as a synonym for the German term and be applied to the same kind of songs in English without prejudice to the scientific "folksong," were it not for its degraded and degrading association with the vulgar music hall ditties. These ditties, which a wise Providence has cursed with the blessing of transientness, have companionship in this study with the so-called "coon songs" and "ragtime tunes" in which some of the elements of the Afro-American folksongs are employed.

Only because I cannot see how a paraphrase would improve it in respect of sententiousness, clearness or comprehensiveness, I make use of a definition which I wrote a decade ago for "The Musical Guide"—a dictionary of terms and much else edited by Rupert Hughes and published by McClure, Phillips & Co.:

Folksong is not popular song in the sense in which the word is most frequently used, but the song of the folk; not only the song admired of the people but, in a strict sense, the song created by the people. It is a body of poetry and music which has come into existence without the influence of conscious art, as a spontaneous utterance, filled with characteristic expression of the feelings of a people. Such songs are marked by certain peculiarities of rhythm, form and melody which are traceable, more or less clearly, to racial (or national) temperament, modes of life, climatic and political conditions, geographical environment and language. Some of these elements, the spiritual, are elusive, but others can be determined and classified.

Though the present purposes are almost purely musical, it will be well to consider that in the folksongs of the world there lies a body of evidence of great value in the study of many things which enter into the science of ethnology, such as racial relations, primitive modes of thought, ancient customs and ancient religions. On this point something shall be said later.

Folksongs are echoes of the heart-beats of the vast folk, and in them are preserved feelings, beliefs and habits of vast antiquity. Not only in the words, which have almost monopolized folksong study thus far, but also in music, and perhaps more truthfully in the music than in the words. Music cannot lie, for the reason that the things which are at its base, the things without which it could not be, are unconscious, unvolitional human products. We act on a recognition of this fact when we judge of the feelings of one with whom we are conversing not so much by what he says to us as by the manner in which he says it. The feelings which sway him publish themselves in the pitch, dynamic intensity and timbre of his voice. Try as we may, if we are powerfully moved we cannot conceal the fact so we open our mouths for utterance. Involuntarily the muscles of the vocal organs contract or relax in obedience to an emotional stimulus, and the drama of feeling playing on the hidden stage of our hearts is betrayed by the *tones* which we utter. These tones, without purpose on our part, have become endowed with the qualities of gravity and acuteness (pitch), loudness and softness (dynamics), and emotional color (timbre), and out of the union and modulation of these elements comes expressive melody. Herbert Spencer has formulated the law: "Feelings are muscular stimuli" and "Variations of voice are the physiological results of variations of feeling." In this lies the simple explanation of the inherent truthfulness and expressiveness of the music which a folk creates for itself.

"The folksong composes itself" (*Das Volkslied dichtet sich selbst*), said Grimm. This is true despite the obvious

[3]

fact that every folksong must once have been the utterance of an individual. What is meant by the axiom is that the creator of the folksong is an unindividualized representative of his people, himself a folk-product. His idioms are taken off the tongue of the people; his subjects are the things which make for the joy and sorrow of the people, and once his song is gone out into the world his identity as its creator is swallowed up in that of the people. Not only is his name forgotten, but his song enters at once upon a series of transformations, which (such is the puissant genius of the people) adapt it to varying circumstances of time and place without loss to its vital loveliness. The creator of a folksong as an individual is a passing phenomenon—like a wave of the sea. His potentiality is racial or national, not personal, and for that reason it is enduring, not ephemeral. As a necessary corollary it follows that the music of the folksong reflects the inner life of the people that gave it birth, and that its characteristics, like the people's physical and mental habits, occupations, methods and feelings are the product of environment, as set forth in the definition.

If Herbert Spencer's physiological analysis of the origin of melody is correct, the finest, because the truest, the most intimate, folk-music is that provoked by suffering. The popular mind does not always think so of music. Its attitude is reflected in the phrase: "Oh, I'm so happy I could sing all day!" But do we sing when we are happy? Song, it is true, is a natural expression of the care-free and light-hearted; but it is oftener an expression of a superficial than a profound feeling. We leap, run, toss our arms, indulge in physical action when in an ecstasy of joy; in sorrow we sit motionless, but, oftener than we are ourselves conscious of the fact, we seek comfort in song. In the popular nomenclature of music the symbols of gayety and gravity are the major and minor moods. It is a broad characterization, and not strictly correct from a scientific point of view; but it serves to point a general rule, the exceptions to which (the Afro-American folksongs forms one of them) invite interesting speculation.

Comparative analysis of the folksongs of widely distributed countries has shown that some peoples are predisposed toward the minor mode, and in some cases explanations of the fact can be found in the geographical, climatic or political conditions under which these peoples have lived in the past or are living now. As a general rule, it will be found that the peoples of high latitudes use the minor mode rather than the major. A study of one hundred songs from every one of twenty-two countries made by Carl Engel,[1] discloses that of the six most predominantly minor countries of Europe five were the most northern ones, his figures being as follows:

	Major	Minor	Mixed
Sweden	14	80	6
Russia	35	52	13
Norway	40	56	4
Wallachia	40	52	8
Denmark	47	52	1
Finland	58	50	2

Melancholy is thus seen to be the characteristic note of Scandinavian music, which reflects the gloom of the fjords and forests and fearful winters of the northern peninsula, where nature makes human life a struggle and death an ever-present though not necessarily terrifying contemplation.

That geographical and climatic conditions are not the only determining factors in the choice of modes is evident, however, from the case of Russia, which extends over nearly 30 degrees of latitude and has so great a variety of climate that the statement that the mean temperature varies from 32 degrees Fahrenheit at Archangel to 58 degrees at Kutais in the Caucasus, conveys only an imperfect notion of the climatic variability of the country. Yet the minor mode is dominant even in the Ukraine.

If an attempt were made, therefore, to divide Europe into major and minor by drawing a line across the map from west to east along the parallel of the 50th degree of latitude the rule would become inoperative as soon as the Russian border was reached. Thence the isomodal line would take a sharp southward trend of no less than 15

[1] See his "Introduction to the Study of National Music."

degrees. All Russia is minor; and Russian folksong, I am prone to think, is the most moving and beautiful folk-music in the world. Other influences than the ordinary are therefore at work here, and their discovery need not detain the reader's mind long. Suffering is suffering, whether it be physical or spiritual, whether it spring from the unfriendliness of nature or the harshness of political and social conditions.

While Russian folksong is thus weighted with sorrow, Russian folkdance is singularly energetic and boisterous. This would seem to present a paradox, but the reason becomes plain when it is remembered that a measured and decorous mode of popular amusement is the normal expression of equable popular life, while wild and desperate gayety is frequently the reaction from suffering. There is a gayety of despair as well as of contentment and happiness. Read this from Dr. Norman McLeod's "Note Book":"My father once saw some emigrants from Lochaber dancing on the deck of an emigrant ship and weeping their eyes out! This feeling is the mother of Irish music. It expresses the struggle of a buoyant, merry heart to get quit of thoughts that often lie too deep for tears. It is the music of an oppressed, conquered, but deeply feeling, impressible, fanciful and generous people. It is for the harp in Tara's halls!"

The rhythms of folksongs may be said to be primarily the product of folkdances, but as these, as a rule, are inspired by the songs which are sung for their regulation, it follows that there is also a verbal basis for rhythms. Whether or not this is true of the rhythmical elements which have entered into Afro-American folksongs cannot be said, for want of knowledge of the languages spoken by the peoples (not people, for they were many and of many kinds) who were brought from Africa to America as slaves. An analogy for the "snap," which is the most pervasive element in the music which came from the Southern plantations (the idiom which has been degraded into "ragtime"), is found in the folk-music of the Magyars of Hungary; and there it is indubitably a product of the poems.

Intervallic peculiarities are more difficult to explain than rhythmic, and are in greater likelihood survivals of primitive elements. Despite its widespread use, the diatonic scale is an artistic or scientific evolution, not an inspiration or a discovery in the natural world of sound; and though it may have existed in primitive music before it became the basis of an art, there was no uniformity in its use. The most idiomatic music of the Finns, who are an older race in the northern European peninsula than any of the Germanic tribes which are their rulers, is confined to the first five tones of the minor scale; old Irish and Scotch songs share the familiar pentatonic scale (by which I mean the modern diatonic series omitting the fourth and seventh steps) with the popular music of China, Japan, Siam and other countries. It is of frequent occurrence in the melodies of the American negroes, and found not infrequently in those of North American Indians; it is probably the oldest tonal system in the world and the most widely dispersed.

César Cui remarks the prevalence in Russia of two major scales, one without the fourth and the other without the third and seventh. Hungarian melodies employ largely the interval called an augmented, or superfluous, second, which is composed of three semitones. The Magyars are Scythians and racially related to the Finns and Turks, and not to their neighbors, the Poles and Russians; yet the same peculiarity is found in Slavic music—in the songs of the Serbs, Bulgarians, Montenegrins and all the other mixed peoples that inhabit the Balkan Peninsula. The idiom is Oriental and a marked feature of the popular and synagogal music of the Jews.

Facts like these indicate the possibility of employing folksong as an aid in the determination of ethnological and ethnographical questions; for its elements have a marvellous tenacity of life. Let this be remembered when the specific study of American folksong is attempted. The persistency of a type of song in spite of a change of environment of sufficient influence to modify the civilization of a people has a convincing illustration in Finland. Though the Finns have mixed with their Germanic neighbors for many

[7]

centuries, there was originally no affinity of race between them and their conquerors. Their origin is in doubt, but it is supposed that they are Mongols and therefore relatives of the Magyars. The influence of the Swedes upon their culture began in the twelfth century, when Christianity was forced upon them, and it has never ceased, though Sweden was compelled by the allied powers to cede Finland to Russia in 1809. Now Russia, though she signed a solemn pact to permit the liberty of language, education and religion to the Finns, is engaged in stamping out the last vestiges of nationalism in the country so beautifully called Suomi by its people.

The active cultivation of music as an art in the modern sense began in Finland toward the close of the eighteenth century, and the composers, directors and teachers were either Germans or Scandinavians educated in Germany. The artistic music of the Finns, therefore, is identified as closely as possible with that of the Scandinavian people, though it has of late received something of a Russian impress; but the vigor and power of primitive influences is attested by the unmistakable elements in the Finnish folksongs. The ancient Finns had the Northern love for music, and their legendary Orpheus was even a more picturesque and potent theurgist than the Greek. His name was Wainamoinen, and when he

> —tuned his lyre with pleasing woe,
> Rivers forgot to run, and winds to blow;
> While listening forests covered, as he played,
> The soft musician in a moving shade.

To Wainamoinen was attributed the invention of the *kantele*, a harp which originally had five strings tuned to the notes which, as has been said, are the basis of the Finnish songs, especially those called *runo* songs, which are still sung. The five-four time which modern composers are now affecting (as is seen in the second movement of Tschaikowsky's "Pathetic" symphony) is an element of the meter of the national Finnish epic, the "Kalevala," whence Longfellow borrowed it for his American epic, "Hiawatha." It, too, is found in many *runo* songs.

[8]

Music is a marvellous conservator. One reason of this is that it is the most efficient of all memory-helps. Another is that among primitive peoples all over the world music became associated with religious worship at so early a period in the development of religion that it acquired even a greater sanctity than words or eucharistic posturing. So the early secular song, as well as the early sacred, is sometimes preserved long after its meaning is forgotten. In this particular, too, folksong becomes an adjunct to ethnology. A striking story is told of how in the middle of the eighteenth century a folksong established fraternal relations between two peoples who had forgotten for centuries that they were of one blood. The tale comes from a French book,[1] but is thus related in an essay on "Some Breton Folksongs," published by Theodore Bacon in "The Atlantic Monthly" for November, 1892:

In September, 1758, an English force effected a descent upon the Breton coast, at Saint-Cast. A company of Lower Bretons, from the neighborhood of Tréguire and Saint-Pol de Léon, was marching against a detachment of Welsh mountaineers, which was coming briskly forward singing a national air, when all at once the Bretons of the French army stopped short in amazement. The air their enemies were singing was one which every day may be heard sounding over the hearths of Brittany. "Electrified," says the historian, grandson himself of an eyewitness, "by accents which spoke to their hearts, they gave way to a sudden enthusiasm, and joined in the same patriotic refrain. The Welsh, in their turn, stood motionless in their ranks. On both sides officers gave the command to fire; but it was in the same language, and the soldiers stood as if petrified. This hesitation continued, however, but a moment: a common emotion was too strong for discipline; the weapons fell from their hands, and the descendants from the ancient Celts renewed upon the battlefield the fraternal ties which had formerly united their fathers."

M. Th. Hersart de la Villemarqué, in his "Barzaz-Breiz," a collection of Breton folksongs, prints two ballads,

[1] "Combat de Saint-Cast, par M. de Saint-Pern Couëlan," 1836.

in one of whlch the battle of Saint-Cast is celebrated, together with two other repulses of English invaders of the Breton coast (at Camaret, in 1486, and Guidel, in 1694). Concerning the encounter at Saint-Cast Villemarqué advances the theory that the singers were the French soldiers, and that the reason why the Welshmen stopped in amazement was that they suspected treachery when they heard their own song. The point is of little consequence, but not so the melody which Villemarqué prints as that to which the old ballad is sung. This, as it appears in "Barzaz-Breiz," is, note for note, the Welsh tune known as "Captain Morgan's March." The same melody is sung to another ballad describing the siege of Guingamp, which took place in 1488. Now, according to Welsh legend, the Morgan whose name is preserved in the ancient *Rhyfelgyrch Cadpen Morgan* was "Captain of the Glamorganshire men, about the year 1294, who gallantly defended his country from the incursion of the Saxons and who dispossessed the Earl of Gloucester of those lands which had formerly been taken from Morgan's forefathers." If the air is as old as that it may well be older still, and, indeed, may have been carried into ancient Armorica by the immigrants from Great Britain who crossed the Channel in large numbers in the fifth and sixth centuries. Other relics of their earlier home besides those of language survive among the people of lower Brittany. Had the soldiers at Saint-Cast sat down together and regaled each other with hero legend and fairy tale they would have found that Arthur and Merlin and the *korrigan* (little fairies) were their common glory and delight. "King Arthur is not dead!" may be heard in Brittany to-day as often as in Cornwall. Moreover, the Welsh song which is sung to the tune of "Captain Morgan's March" and the Breton ballad "Emgann Sant-Kast"[1] have one vigorous sentiment in common: "Cursed be the Saxon!"

[1] See Appendix.

CHAPTER II

SONGS OF THE AMERICAN SLAVES

ORIGINALITY OF THE AFRO-AMERICAN FOLKSONGS—
DR. WALLASCHEK AND HIS CONTENTION—EXTENT
OF IMITATIONS IN THE SONGS—ALLUSIONS
TO SLAVERY—HOW THE SONGS GREW—
ARE THEY ENTITLED TO BE CALLED
AMERICAN?—THE NEGRO IN
AMERICAN HISTORY.

It would never have occurred to me to undertake to prove the existence of genuine folksongs in America, and those the songs which were created by the black slaves of the Southern States, if the fact of such existence had not been denied by at least one writer who has affected the scientific manner, and it had not become the habit of a certain class of writers in this country, while conceding the interesting character of the songs, to refuse them the right to be called American. A foolish pride on the part of one class of Americans of more or less remote English ancestry, and a more easily understood and more pardonable prejudice on the part of former slaveholders and their descendants, might explain this attitude in New England and the South, but why a foreign writer, with whom a personal equation should not have been in any degree operative, should have gone out of his way to pronounce against the originality of the songs of the American negroes, cannot be so readily understood. Yet, in his book, "Primitive Music,"[1] Dr. Richard Wallaschek says:

There still remains to be mentioned one race which is spread all over America and whose musical powers have attracted the attention of many Europeans—the negro race. It may seem inappropriate to treat of the negroes in this place, but it is of their capabilities under the influence of culture that I wish to make a few remarks. I think I may say that, generally speaking, these negro songs are very much overrated, and that, as a rule, they are mere imitations of European compositions which the negroes have picked up and served up again with slight variations. Moreover, it is a remarkable

[1] "An Inquiry into the Origin and Development of Music, Songs, Instruments, Dances and Pantomines of Savage Races" (London, 1893).

[11]

fact that one author has frequently copied his praise of negro songs from another, and determined from it the great capabilities of the blacks, when a closer examination would have revealed the fact that they were not musical songs at all, but merely simple poems. This is undoubtedly the case with the oft quoted negro songs of Day and Busch. The latter declares that the lucrative business which negroes made by singing their songs in the streets of American towns determined the whites to imitate them, and with blackened faces to perform their own "compositions" as negro songs. We must be on our guard against the selections of so-called negro songs, which are often offered us as negro compositions.

Miss McKim and Mr. Spaulding were the first to try to make negro songs known, the former of whom, in connection with Allen and Ware, published a large collection which for the most part had been got together by the negroes of Coffin's point and in the neighboring plantations at St. Helena. I cannot think that these and the rest of the songs deserve the praise given by the editors, for they are unmistakably "arranged"—not to say ignorantly borrowed—from the national songs of all nations, from military signals, well-known marches, German student songs, etc., unless it is pure accident which has caused me to light upon traces of so many of them. Miss McKim herself says it is difficult to reproduce in notes their peculiar guttural sounds and rhythmical effects—almost as difficult, in fact as with the songs of birds or the tones of an æolian harp. "Still, the greater part of negro music is civilized in its character," sometimes influenced by the whites, sometimes directly imitated. After this we may forego the necessity for a thorough examination, although it must be mentioned here, because the songs are so often given without more ado as examples of primitive music. It is, as a matter of fact, no longer primitive, even in its wealth of borrowed melody. Feeling for harmony seems fairly developed.

It was not Miss McKim, but Mr. Allen, who called attention to the "civilized" character of the music of the slaves. In what Miss McKim said about the difficulty of reproducing "the entire character" of the music, as she expresses it, by the conventional symbols of the art, she adduces a proof of the primitive nature of some of its elements. The study of these elements might profitably have occupied Dr. Wallaschek's attention for a space. Had he made more than cursory examination of them he would not have been so sweeping in his characterization of the songs as mere imitations. The authors whom he quotes[1] wrote before a collection of songs of the American negroes had been made on which a scientific, critical opinion might be based. As for Dr. Wallaschek, his critical attitude toward "Slave Songs" is amply shown by his bracketing it with a publication of Christy minstrel songs which appeared in London; his method is illustrated by

[1] Charles William Day, who published a work entitled "Five Years' Residence in the West Indies," in 1852, and Moritz Busch, who in 1854 published his "Wanderungen zwischen Hudson und Mississippi."

his acceptance in his résumé of the observations of travellers among savage peoples (an extremely helpful book
otherwise) of their terminology as well as their opinions
in musical matters. Now, nothing is more notorious than
that the overwhelming majority of the travellers who have
written about primitive peoples have been destitute of
even the most elemental knowledge of practical as well
as theoretical music; yet without some knowledge of the
art it is impossible even to give an intelligent description
of the rudest musical instruments. The phenomenon is
not peculiar to African travellers, though the confusion
of terms and opinions is greater, perhaps, in books on
Africa than anywhere else. Dr. Wallaschek did not permit the fact to embarrass him in the least, nor did he even
attempt to set the writers straight so far as properly to
classify the instruments which they describe. All kinds
of instruments of the stringed kind are jumbled higgledy-
piggledy in these descriptions, regardless of whether or
not they had fingerboards or belonged to the harp family;
bamboo instruments are called flutes, even if they are
sounded by being struck; wooden gongs are permitted to
parade as drums, and the universal "whizzer," or "buzzer"
(a bit of flat wood attached to a string and made to give
a whirring sound by being whirled through the air) is
treated even by Dr. Wallaschek as if it were an æolian
harp. A common African instrument of rhythm, a stick
with one edge notched like a saw, over which another
stick is rubbed, which has its counterpart in Louisiana in
the jawbone and key, is discussed as if it belonged to the
viol family, simply because it is rubbed. He does not
challenge even so infantile a statement as that of Captain
John Smith when he asserts that the natives of Virginia
had "bass, tenor, counter-tenor, alto and soprano rattles."
And so on. These things may not influence Dr. Wallaschek's deductions, but they betoken a carelessness of
mind which should not exist in a scientific investigator, and
justify a challenge of his statement that the songs of the
American negroes are predominantly borrowings from
European music.

Besides, the utterance is illogical. Similarities exist between the folksongs of all peoples. Their overlapping is a necessary consequence of the proximity and intermingling of peoples, like modifications of language; and there are some characteristics which all songs except those of the rudest and most primitive kind must have in common. The prevalence of the diatonic scales and the existence of march-rhythms, for instance, make parallels unavoidable. If the use of such scales and rhythms in the folksongs of the American negroes is an evidence of plagiarism or imitation, it is to be feared that the peoples whose music they put under tribute have been equally culpable with them. Again, if the songs are but copies of "the national songs of all nations, military signals, well-known marches, German student songs, etc.," why did white men blacken their faces and imitate these imitations? Were the facilities of the slaves to hear all these varieties of foreign music better than those of their white imitators? It is plain that Dr. Wallaschek never took the trouble to acquaint himself with the environment of the black slaves in the United States. How much music containing the exotic elements which I have found in some songs, and which I shall presently discuss, ever penetrated to the plantations where these songs grew? It did not need Dr. Wallaschek's confession that he did not think it necessary to make a thorough examination of even the one genuine collection which came under his notice to demonstrate that he did not look analytically at the songs as a professedly scientific man should have done before publishing his wholesale characterization and condemnation. This characterization is of a piece with his statement that musical contests which he mentions of the Nishian women which are "won by the woman who sings loudest and longest" are "still in use in America," which precious piece of intelligence he proves by relating a newspaper story about a pianoforte playing match in a dime museum in New York in 1892. The truth is that, like many another complacent German savant, Dr. Wallaschek thinks Americans are barbarians. He is welcome to his opinion, which can harm no one but himself.

SONGS OF THE AMERICAN SLAVES

That there should be resemblances between some of the
songs sung by the American blacks and popular songs of
other origin need surprise no one. In the remark about
civilized music made by Mr. Allen, which Dr. Wallaschek
attributes to Miss McKim, it is admitted that the music
of the negroes is "partly actually imitated from their
music," *i. e.*, the music of the whites; but Mr. Allen adds:
"In the main it appears to be original in the best sense
of the word, and the more we examine the subject, the
more genuine it appears to be. In a very few songs, as
Nos. 19, 23 and 25, strains of familiar tunes are readily
traced; and it may easily be that others contain strains
of less familiar music which the slaves heard their masters
sing or play." It would be singular, indeed, if this were
not the case, for it is a universal law. Of the songs singled
out by Mr. Allen, No. 19 echoes what Mr. Allen describes
as a familiar Methodist hymn, 'Ain't I glad I got out of
the Wilderness,'" but he admits that it may be original. I
have never seen the song in a collection of Methodist
hymns, but I am certain that I used to sing it as a boy to
words which were anything but religious. Moreover, the
second period of the tune, the only part that is in controversy, has a prototype of great dignity and classic
ancestry; it is the theme of the first Allegro of Bach's
sonata in E for violin and clavier. I know of no parallel
for No. 23 ("I saw the Beam in my Sister's eye") except
in other negro songs. The second period of No. 23 ("Gwine
Follow"), as Mr. Allen observes, "is evidently 'Buffalo,'
variously known as 'Charleston' or 'Baltimore Gals.'"
But who made the tune for the "gals" of Buffalo, Charleston
and Baltimore? The melodies which were more direct
progenitors of the songs which Christy's Minstrels and
other minstrel companies carried all over the land were
attributed to the Southern negroes; songs like "Coal-
black Rose," "Zip Coon" and "Ole Virginny Nebber
Tire," have always been accepted as the creations of the
blacks, though I do not know whether or not they really
are. Concerning them I am skeptical, to say the least,
if only for the reason that we have no evidence on the sub-

[15]

ject. So-called negro songs are more than a century old in the music-rooms of America. A song descriptive of the battle of Plattsburg was sung in a drama to words supposedly in negro dialect, as long ago as 1815. "Jump Jim Crow" was caught by Thomas D. ("Daddy") Rice from the singing and dancing of an old, deformed and decrepit negro slave in Louisville eighty-five years ago (if the best evidence obtainable on the subject is to be believed), and this was the starting-point of negro minstrelsy of the Christy type. "Dandy Jim of Caroline" may also have had a negro origin; I do not know, and the question is inconsequential here for the reason that the Afro-American folksongs which I am trying to study owe absolutely nothing to the songs which the stage impersonators of the negro slave made popular in the United States and England. They belong to an entirely different order of creations. For one thing, they are predominantly religious songs; it is a singular fact that very few secular songs—those which are referred to as "reel tunes," "fiddle songs," "corn songs" and "devil songs," for which the slaves generally expressed a deep abhorrence, though many of them, no doubt, were used to stimulate them while at work in the fields—have been preserved, while "shout songs" and other "speritchils" (spirituals—"ballets" they were called at a later day) have been kept alive by the hundreds. The explanation of the phenomenon is psychological.

There are a few other resemblances which may be looked into. "Who is on the Lord's side?"[1] may have suggested the notion of "military calls" to Dr. Wallaschek. "In Bright Mansions Above"[2] contains a phrase which may have been inspired by "The Wearing of the Green." A palpable likeness to "Camptown Races" exists in "Lord, Remember Me."[3] Stephen C. Foster wrote "Camptown Races" in 1850; the book called "Slave Songs of the United States" was published in 1867, but the songs were collected several years before. I have no desire to rob

[1] "Slave Songs," No. 75.
[2] No. 78 of the Fisk Jubilee Collection
[3] No. 7 in "Slave Songs"

Foster of the credit of having written the melody of his song; he would have felt justified had he taken it from the lips of a slave, but it is more than likely that he invented it and that it was borrowed in part for a hymn by the negroes. The "spirituals" are much sophisticated with worldly sentiment and phrase.

There are surprisingly few references to the servitude of the blacks in their folksongs which can be traced to ante-bellum days. The text of "Mother, is Massa Gwine to sell us To-morrow?" would seem to be one of these; but it is not in the earliest collection and may be of later date in spite of its sentiment. I present three interesting examples which celebrate the deliverance from slavery, of which two, "Many Thousands Gone"[1] and "Many Thousand Go"[2] are obviously musical variants of the same song (see pages 18, 19, 20). Colonel Higginson, who collected the second, says of it in his "Atlantic Monthly" essay: "They had another song to which the Rebellion had actually given rise. This was composed by nobody knew whom—though it was the most recent, doubtless, of all these 'spirituals'—and had been sung in secret to avoid detection. It is certainly plaintive enough. The peck of corn and pint of salt were slavery's rations." The editors of "Slave Songs" add: "Lieutenant-Colonel Trowbridge learned that it was first sung when Beauregard took the slaves to the islands to build the fortifications at Hilton Head and Bay Point." The third song, "Done wid Driber's Dribin'," was first printed in Mr. H. G. Spaulding's essay "Under the Palmetto" in the "Continental Monthly" for August, 1863. The song "Oh, Freedom over Me," which Dr. Burghardt du Bois quotes in his "The Souls of Black Folk" as an expression of longing for deliverance from slavery encouraged by fugitive slaves and the agitation of free negro leaders before the War of the Rebellion, challenges no interest for its musical contents, since it is a compound of two white men's tunes—"Lily Dale," a sentimental ditty, and "The Battle-Cry of Freedom," a patriotic song composed by George F. Root, in

[1] Fisk Jubilee Collection, No. 23
[2] "Slave Songs," No. 64

[17]

THREE EMANCIPATION SONGS

I. Words and Melody from "Slave Songs of the United States";—II. From "The Continental Monthly" of August, 1863, reprinted in "Slave Songs";— III. From "The Story of the Jubilee Singers." The arrangements are by H. T. Burleigh.

Many Thousand Go

I

2. No more driver's lash for me.
3. No more pint o' salt for me.
4. No more hundred lash for me.
5. No more mistress' call for me.

Done wid Driber's Dribin'

II

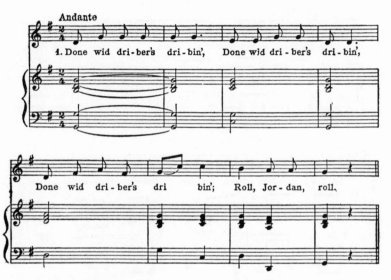

1. Done wid dri-ber's dri-bin', Done wid dri-ber's dri-bin',

Done wid dri-ber's dri bin'; Roll, Jor-dan, roll.

2. Done wid Massa's hollerin',
   Done wid Massa's hollerin',
   Done wid Massa's hollerin';
   Roll, Jordan, roll.

3. Done wid Missus' scoldin',
   Done wid Missus' scoldin',
   Done wid Missus' scoldin';
   Roll, Jordan, roll.

Many Thousands Gone
III

2. No more peck o' corn, etc.   4. No more pint o' salt, etc.

3. No more driver's lash, etc.   5. No more hundred lash, etc.

6. No more mistress' call, etc.

Chicago, and inspired by President Lincoln's second call for volunteers in the summer of 1861. There was time for the negro song to have grown up between 1861 and the emancipation of the slaves, but it is not likely that slaves anywhere in the United States outside of the lines of the Federal armies would have dared to sing

> O Freedom, O Freedom,
> O Freedom over me!
> Before I'll be a slave.
> I'll be buried in my grave,
> And go home to my Lord,
> And be free!

before 1863. Besides, the song did not appear in print, I believe, till it was published in "Religious Folk Songs of the Negro, as Sung on the Plantations," an edition of "Cabin and Plantation Songs as Sung by the Hampton Students," published in 1909. The early editions of the book knew nothing of the song. Colonel Higginson quotes a song with a burden of "We'll soon be free," for singing which negroes had been put in jail at the outbreak of the Rebellion in Georgetown, S. C. In spite of the obviously apparent sentiment, Colonel Higginson says it had no reference to slavery, though he thinks it may have been sung "with redoubled emphasis during the new events." It was, in fact, a song of hoped-for deliverance from the sufferings of this world and of anticipation of the joys of Paradise, where the faithful were to "walk de miry road" and "de golden streets," on which pathways "pleasure never dies." No doubt there was to the singers a hidden allegorical significance in the numerous allusions to the deliverance of the Israelites from Egyptian bondage contained in the songs, and some of this significance may have crept into the songs before the day of freedom began to dawn. A line, "The Lord will call us home," in the song just referred to, Colonel Higginson says "was evidently thought to be a symbolical verse; for, as a little drummer-boy explained to me, showing all his white teeth as he sat in the moonlight by the door of my tent, 'Dey tink de Lord mean for say de Yankees.' "

If the songs which came from the plantations of the

South are to conform to the scientific definition of folksongs as I laid it down in the preceding chapter, they must be "born, not made;" they must be spontaneous utterances of the people who originally sang them; they must also be the fruit of the creative capacity of a whole and ingenuous people, not of individual artists, and give voice to the joys, sorrows and aspirations of that people. They must betray the influences of the environment in which they sprang up, and may preserve relics of the likes and aptitudes of their creators when in the earlier environment from which they emerged. The best of them must be felt by the singers themselves to be emotional utterances. The only considerable body of song which has come into existence in the territory now compassed by the United States, I might even say in North America, excepting the primitive songs of the Indians (which present an entirely different aspect), are the songs of the former black slaves. In Canada the songs of the people, or that portion of the people that can be said still to sing from impulse, are predominantly French, not only in language but in subject. They were for the greater part transferred to this continent with the bodily integrity which they now possess. Only a small portion show an admixture of Indian elements; but the songs of the black slaves of the South are original and native products. They contain idioms which were transplanted hither from Africa, but as songs they are the product of American institutions; of the social, political and geographical environment within which their creators were placed in America; of the influences to which they were subjected in America; of the joys, sorrows and experiences which fell to their lot in America.

Nowhere save on the plantations of the South could the emotional life which is essential to the development of true folksong be developed; nowhere else was there the necessary meeting of the spiritual cause and the simple agent and vehicle. The white inhabitants of the continent have never been in the state of cultural ingenuousness which prompts spontaneous emotional utterance in music.

[22]

Civilization atrophies the faculty which creates this phenomenon as it does the creation of myth and legend. Sometimes the faculty is galvanized into life by vast calamities or crises which shake all the fibres of social and national existence; and then we see its fruits in the compositions of popular musicians. Thus the War of the Rebellion produced songs markedly imbued with the spirit of folksong, like "The Battle-Cry of Freedom," "Tramp, Tramp, Tramp, the Boys are Marching," and "Marching Through Georgia." But it is a singular fact that the patriotic songs of the American people during the War of the Revolution and the War of 1812 were literary and musical parodies of English songs. We took the music of "Yankee Doodle" and "The Star-Spangled Banner" from the lips of the enemy.

It did not lie in the nature of the mill life of New England or the segregated agricultural life of the Western pioneers to inspire folksongs; those occupations lacked the romantic and emotional elements which existed in the slave life of the plantations in the South and which invited celebration in song—grave and gay. Nor were the people of the North possessed of the ingenuous, native musical capacity of the Southern blacks.

It is in the nature of things that the origin of individual folksongs should as a rule remain unknown; but we have evidence to show how some of them grew, and from it we deduce the general rule as it has been laid down. Colonel Thomas Wentworth Higginson, in his delightful essay "Negro Spirituals," published in "The Atlantic Monthly" for June, 1867, tells an illuminative anecdote. Speaking of "No More Peck of Corn for Me," he says:

Even of this last composition, however, we have only the approximate date, and know nothing of the mode of composition. Allen Ramsey says of the Scotch songs that, no matter who made them, they were soon attributed to the minister of the parish whence they sprang. And I always wondered, about these, whether they had always a conscious and definite origin in some leading mind or whether they grew by gradual accretion in an almost unconscious way. On this point I could get no information, though I asked many questions, until at last one day when I was being rowed across from Beaufort to Ladies' Island, I found myself, with delight, on the actual trail of a song. One of the oarsmen, a brisk young fellow, not a soldier, on being asked for his theory of the matter, dropped out a coy confession. "Some good sperituals," he said, "are start jest out o' curiosity. I bin a-raise a sing myself once."

My dream was fulfilled, and I had traced out not the poem alone, but the poet. I implored him to proceed.

"Once we boys went for tote some rice, and de nigger driver, he keep a-callin' on us: and I say, 'O, de ole nigger driver!'" Den anudder said, 'Fust t'ing my mammy tole me was not'in' so bad as a nigger driver.' Den I made a sing, just puttin' a word and den anudder word."

Then he began singing and the men, after listening a moment, joined in the chorus as if it were an old acquaintance, though they evidently had never heard it before. I saw how easily a new "sing" took root among them.

"O, de ole nigger driver!
O, gwine away!
Fust t'ing my mammy tell me.
O, gwine away!
Tell me 'bout de nigger driver,
O, gwine away!
Nigger driver second devil,
O, gwine away!
Best t'ing for do he driver,
O, gwine away!
Knock he down and spoil he labor—
O, gwine away!

A similar story, which also throws light on the emancipation songs which I have printed, was told by J. Miller McKim in an address delivered in Philadelphia on July 9, 1862:

I asked one of these blacks, one of the most intelligent of them, where they got these songs.

"Dey make 'em, sah."

"How do they make them?"

After a pause, evidently casting about for an explanation, he said:

"I'll tell you; it's dis way: My master call me up an' order me a short peck of corn and a hundred lash. My friends see it and is sorry for me. When dey come to de praise meeting dat night dey sing about it. Some's very good singers and know how; and dey work it in, work it in, you know, till dey get it right; and dat's de way."

"In ancient Rome sick slaves were exposed on the island of Aesculapius, in the Tiber; by a decree of Claudius slaves so exposed could not be reclaimed by their master."—(Encyclopædia Britannica, art. "Slavery.")

An incident which gave rise in Jamaica to a folksong, which is a remarkably fine example of dramatic directness and forcefulness, but of which, most unfortunately, the music has not been preserved, recalls this ancient regulation. Here is the song:

"Take him to the gully! Take him to the gully,
But bringee back the frock and the board."
"O massa, massa! Me no deadee yet!"
"Take him to the gully! Take him to the gully;
Carry him along!"

How this song came into existence is thus related in

"A Journal of a Residence Among the Negroes in the West Indies," by Matthew Gregory Lewis:[1]

The song alludes to a transaction which took place about fifty years ago on an estate called Spring Garden, the owner of which is quoted as the cruelest proprietor that ever disgraced Jamaica. It was his constant practice, whenever a sick negro was pronounced incurable, to order the poor wretch to be carried to a solitary vale upon his estate, called the Gully, where he was thrown down and abandoned to his fate—which fate was generally to be half-devoured by the john crows before death had put an end to his sufferings. By this proceeding the avaricious owner avoided the expense of maintaining the slave during his last illness; and in order that he might be as little a loser as possible he always enjoined the negro bearers of the dying man to strip him naked before leaving the Gully, and not to forget to bring back his frock and the board on which he had been carried down.

One poor creature, while in the act of being removed, screamed out most piteously that he was not dead yet, and implored not to be left to perish in the Gully in a manner so horrible. His cries had no effect upon the master, but operated so forcibly on the less marble hearts of his fellow slaves that in the night some of them removed him back to the negro village privately and nursed him there with so much care that he recovered and left the estate unquestioned and undiscovered. Unluckily, one day the master was passing through Kingston, when, on turning the corner of a street suddenly, he found himself face to face with the negro whom he had supposed long ago to have been picked to the bones in the Gully. He immediately seized him, claimed him as his slave and ordered his attendants to convey him to his house; but the fellow's cry attracted a crowd around them before he could be dragged away. He related his melancholy story and the singular manner in which he had recovered his life and liberty, and the public indignation was so forcibly excited by the shocking tale that Mr. B—— was glad to save himself from being torn to pieces by a precipitate retreat from Kingston and never ventured to advance his claim to the negro a second time.

But the story lived in the song which the narrator heard half a century later. Imagine the dramatic pathos of the words paired with the pathos of the tune which welled up with them when the singers repeated the harsh utterances of the master and the pleadings of the wretched slave! It is out of experiences like these that folksongs are made. There were, it is true, few cases of such monstrous cruelty in any of the sections in which slavery flourished in America, though it fell to my lot fifteen years after slavery had been abolished to report the testimony in a law case of an old black woman who was seeking to recover damages from a former Sheriff of Kenton County, Ky., for having abducted her, when a free woman living in Cincinnati, and selling her into slavery. A slave she remained until freed by President Lincoln's proclamation, and in measure of damages she told on the witness stand of

[1] London, 1845.

seeing a young black woman on a plantation in Mississippi stripped naked, tied by the feet and hands flat upon the ground and so inhumanly flogged that she died in a few hours. That story also might well have been perpetuated in a folksong. There was sunshine as well as gloom in the life of the black slaves in the Southern colonies and States, and so we have songs which are gay as well as grave; but as a rule the finest songs are the fruits of suffering undergone and the hope of the deliverance from bondage which was to come with translation to heaven after death. The oldest of them are the most beautiful, and many of the most striking have never yet been collected, partly because they contained elements, melodic as well as rhythmical, which baffled the ingenuity of the early collectors. Unfortunately, trained musicians have never entered upon the field, and it is to be feared that it is now too late. The peculiarities which the collaborators on "Slave Songs of the United States" recognized, but could not imprison on the written page, were elements which would have been of especial interest to the student of art.

Is it not the merest quibble to say that these songs are not American? They were created in America under American influences and by people who are Americans in the same sense that any other element of our population is American—every element except the aboriginal. But is there an aboriginal element? Are the red men autochthones? Science seems to have answered that they are not. Then they, too, are American only because they have come to live in America. They may have come from Asia. The majority of other Americans came from Europe. Is it only an African who can sojourn here without becoming an American and producing American things? Is it a matter of length of stay in the country? Scarcely that; or some negroes would have at least as good a claim on the title as the descendants of the Puritans and Pilgrims. Negroes figure in the accounts of his voyages to America made by Columbus. Their presence in the West Indies was noticed as early as 1501. Balboa was assisted by negroes in building the first ships sent into the Pacific

Ocean from American shores. A year before the English colonists landed on Plymouth Rock negroes were sold into servitude in Virginia. When the first census of the United States was taken in 1790, there were 757,208 negroes in the country. There are now 10,000,000. These people all speak the language of America. They are native born. Their songs, a matter of real moment in the controversy, are sung in the language of America (albeit in a corrupt dialect), and as much entitled to be called American songs as would be the songs, were there any such, created here by any other element of our population. They may not give voice to the feelings of the entire population of the country, but for a song which shall do that we shall have to wait until the amalgamation of the inhabitants of the United States is complete. Will such a time ever come? Perhaps so; but it will be after the people of the world cease swarming as they have swarmed from the birth of history till now. There was a travelled road from Mesopotamia to the Pillars of Hercules in the time of Abraham. The women of Mykæne wore beads of amber brought from the German Ocean, when

"Ilion, like a mist, rose into towers."

The folksongs of Suabia, Bavaria, the Rhineland, Franconia—of all the German countries, principalities and provinces—are German folksongs; the songs of the German apprentices, soldiers, huntsmen, clerks, journeymen—giving voice to the experiences and feelings of each group—are all German folksongs. Why are not the songs of the American negroes American folksongs? Can any one say? It is deplorable that so pessimistic a note should sound through the writings of any popular champion as sounds through the most eloquent English book ever written by any one of African blood; but no one shall read Burghardt DuBois's "The Souls of Black Folk" without being moved by the pathos of his painful cry:

Your country? How came it yours? Before the Pilgrims landed we were here. Here we have brought our three gifts and mingled them with yours—a gift of story and song, soft, stirring melody in an ill harmonized and unmelodious land; the gift of sweat and brawn to beat back the wilderness, conquer the soil and lay the foundations of this vast economic empire two hundred years earlier than your weak hands could have done it; the third, a gift of the Spirit. Around us the history of the land has centered for thrice a hundred years; out of the nation's heart we have called all that was best to throttle and subdue all that was worst; fire and blood, prayer and sacrifice, have billowed over this people, and they have found peace only in the altars of the God of Right. Nor has our gift of the Spirit been merely passive. Actively we have woven ourselves with the very warp and woof of this nation —we fought their battles, shared their sorrows, mingled our blood with theirs, and generation after generation have pleaded with a headstrong, careless people to despise not Justice, Mercy and Truth, lest the nation be smitten with a curse. Our song, our toil, our cheer and warning have been given to this nation in blood brotherhood. Are not these gifts worth giving? Is not this work and striving? Would America have been America without her negro people?

Even so is the hope that sang in the songs of my fathers well sung. If somewhere in this swirl and chaos of things there dwells Eternal Good, pitiful yet masterful, then anon in His good time America shall rend the veil and the prisoned shall go free—free, free as the sunshine trickling down the morning into these high windows of mine; free as yonder fresh voices welling up to me from the caverns of brick and mortar below—swelling with song, instinct with life, tremulous treble and darkening bass.

Greatly as it pains me, I should be sorry if one should ask me to strike that passage out of "American" prose writing.

CHAPTER III

RELIGIOUS CHARACTER
OF THE SONGS

The Paucity of Secular Songs among the Slaves—
Campmeetings, "Spirituals" and "Shouts"—
Work-Songs of the Fields and Rivers—
Lafcadio Hearn and Negro Music—
African Relics and Voodoo Cere-
monies.

Having looked into the genesis of the folksongs of the
American negroes, I purpose now to lay a foundation for
examination into some of the musical idioms which charac-
terize them, so that, presently, their origin as well as their
effect may be discussed. Before then, however, something
must be said about the various classes of songs and their
use. Here the most striking fact that presents itself is
the predominance of hymns, or religious songs. The reason
for this will readily be found by those who are willing
to accept Herbert Spencer's theory of the origin of music
and my definition of folksong. Slavery was the sorrow
of the Southern blacks; religion was their comfort and
refuge. That religion was not a dogmatic, philosophical
or even ethical system so much as it was an emotional
experience. "These hymns," says Mr. Allen in his introduction to "Slave Songs of the United States," "will be
found peculiarly interesting in illustrating the feelings,
opinions and habits of the slaves. . . . One of their
customs, often alluded to in the songs, . . . is that of
wandering through the woods and swamps when under
religious excitement, like the ancient bacchantes." "Almost all their songs were thoroughly religious in their
tone," says Colonel Higginson, "and were in a minor key,
both as to words and music. The attitude is always the
same, and, as a commentary on the life of the race, is
infinitely pathetic. Nothing but patience for this life—

[29]

nothing but triumph in the next. Sometimes the present predominates, sometimes the future; but the combination is always implied."[1]

"Though the words are sometimes rude and the strains often wild, yet they are the outpourings of an ignorant and poverty-stricken people, whose religious language and ideals struggled for expression and found it through limited vocabularies and primitive harmonies. They are not merely poetry, they are life itself—the life of the human soul manifesting itself in rude words, wild strains and curious, though beautiful harmonies," says Robert R. Moton, commandant of Hampton Institute. Booker T. Washington bears this testimony: "The negro folksong has for the negro race the same value that the folksong of any other people has for that people. It reminds the race of the 'rock whence it was hewn,' it fosters race pride, and in the days of slavery it furnished an outlet for the anguish of smitten hearts. . . . The plantation songs known as the 'spirituals' are the spontaneous outbursts of intense religious fervor, and had their origin chiefly in the camp-meetings, the revivals, and in other religious exercises. They breathe a childlike faith in a personal Father and glow with the hope that the children of bondage will ultimately pass out of the wilderness of slavery into the land of freedom."

Writing in "The Century Magazine" for August, 1899, Marion Alexander Haskell said: "The musical talent of the uneducated negro finds almost its only expression in religious song, and for this there is a simple explanation. A race strongly imbued with religious sentiment, one rarely finds among them an adult who has not gone through that emotional experience known as conversion, after which it is considered vanity and sinfulness to indulge in song other than that of a sacred character. The new-found child

[1] Concerning the prevalent mode of the songs Colonel Higginson is in error; they are predominantly major, not minor. The mistake is a common one among persons who have no technical training in music and who have been taught that suffering always expresses itself in the minor mode. A great majority of those who write about savage or primitive music generally set it down as minor whenever it has a melancholy cast.

You May Bury Me in the East

hear the trumpet sound   In that morn-ing.   In that morn-ing, my Lord,

How I long to go for to   hear the trumpet sound in that morn-ing.

2. Father Gabriel in that day,
   He'll take wings and fly away,
   For to hear the trumpet sound
     In that morning, etc.
   You may bury him, etc.

3. Good old Christians in that day,
   They'll take wings and fly away,
     etc.

4. Good old preachers in that day,
   They'll take wings, etc.

5. In that dreadful judgment-day
   I'll take wings, etc.

Arranged for men's voices for the Mendelssohn Glee Club of New York by Arthur Mees; published here by permission.

[31]

of the church knows but little of that which he must forgo, for his mother before him sang only spirituals, and to these he naturally turns as to old friends whom his own religious experiences have clothed in new dignity and light."

There is nothing strange in the fact that the original collectors of slave songs and later students of slave life in America should thus recognize the psychological origin of negro song, for they were familiar with the phenomena which accompanied it; but it is worthy of note that a foreigner, who approached the subject on its scientific and artistic side only and to whom all such phenomena must have seemed strange, should have been equally apprecia-tive. In his monograph, "La Musique chez les Peuples indigènes de l'Amérique du Nord," M. Julien Tiersot, after describing a campmeeting as he had learned to know it from the descriptions of others, says:

> It is indubitable, as all who have made a special study of the question agree, that it is in these superheated religious assemblies that the most genuine (*plus clair*) songs in the negro repertory had their origin. They use them on all occasions. Like all peoples of low culture, the negroes accompany their manual labors with song. Noteworthy are the "corn songs," which are sung in the harvest season to stimulate the gathering of the grain. The efficiency of these songs is so well recognized that the owners of the plantations pay extra wages to singers capable of leading the chorus of laborers. These songs, however, have no distinctive character; they are religious hymns. The same holds true of the songs sung by negroes for their diversion, when at rest in their cabins, in the family circle or for the dance. Such a use need not surprise us when we have seen their religious meetings degenerate into dishevelled dances under the influence of the same songs. It is the hymn which must sanctify the dance. Carefully do they guard it against any admixture of the profane element! A superstitous dread in this regard is another convincing proof of how completely they have forgotten their African origin. They would believe themselves damned were they to repeat the songs of paganism; to do this would, in their eyes, be to commit original and unpardonable sin.

The "dishevelled dance" to which M. Tiersot alludes is the "shout" which in the days of slavery flourished chiefly in South Carolina and the States south of it. "It appears to be found in Florida," says Mr. Allen in his preface to "Slave Songs," but not in North Carolina or Virginia." I have a hymn taken down from the lips of an old slave woman in Kentucky which the collector[1] designated as a "shout," and it is probable that the custom was more widely extended than Mr. Allen and his collabora-

[1] Miss Mildred J. Hill, of Louisville, to whom I am indebted for several interesting specimens.

tors, who gleaned chiefly in South Carolina and the Gulf States, knew. Mr. Allen refers to the fact that the term "shouting" is used in Virginia "in reference to a peculiar motion of the body not wholly unlike the Carolina shouting." Very keenly he surmises, too, that it "is not unlikely that this remarkable religious ceremony is a relic of some native African dance, as the Romaïka is of the classic Pyrrhic." A secular parody of it can easily be recalled by all persons who remember the old-fashioned minstrel shows, for it was perpetuated in the so-called "walk-around" of those entertainments. "Dixie," which became the war-song of the Southrons during the War of the Rebellion, was written by Dan Emmet as a "walk-around" for Bryant's Minstrels in 1859. I shall let an eyewitness describe the "shout." It is a writer in "The Nation" of May 30, 1867:

There is a ceremony which the white clergymen are inclined to discountenance, and even of the colored elders some of the more discreet try sometimes to put on a face of discouragement; and, although if pressed for Biblical warrant for the "shout," they generally seem to think, "he in de Book," or, "he dere-da in Matchew," still it is not considered blasphemous or improper if "de chillen" and "dem young gal" carry it on in the evening for amusement's sake, and with no well-defined intention of "praise." But the true "shout" takes place on Sundays, or on "praise" nights through the week, and either in the praise-house or in some cabin in which a regular religious meeting has been held. Very likely more than half the population of a plantation is gathered together. Let it be the evening, and a light wood fire burns red before the door of the house and on the hearth. For some time one can hear, though at a good distance, the vociferous exhortation or prayer of the presiding elder or of the brother who has a gift that way and is not "on the back seat"—a phrase the interpretation of which is "under the censure of the church authorities for bad behavior"—and at regular intervals one hears the elder "deaconing" a hymnbook hymn, which is sung two lines at a time and whose wailing cadences, borne on the night air, are indescribably melancholy.

But the benches are pushed back to the wall when the formal meeting is over, and old and young, men and women, sprucely dressed young men, grotesquely half-clad field hands—the women generally with gay handkerchiefs twisted about their heads and with short skirts—boys with tattered shirts and men's trousers, young girls bare-footed, all stand up in the middle of the floor, and when the "sperichil" is struck up begin first walking and by and by shuffling around, one after the other, in a ring. The foot is hardly taken from the floor, and the progression is mainly due to a jerking, hitching motion which agitates the entire shouter and soon brings out streams of perspiration. Sometimes they dance silently, sometimes as they shuffle they sing the chorus of the spiritual, and sometimes the song itself is also sung by the dancers. But more frequently a band, composed of some of the best singers and of tired shouters, stand at the side of the room to "base" the others, singing the body of the song and clapping their hands together or on the knees. Song and dance are alike extremely energetic, and often, when the shout lasts into the middle of the night, the monotonous thud, thud of the feet prevents sleep within half a mile of the praise-house.

[33]

The editors of "Slave Songs" were liberal-minded persons, who, though engaged in philanthropic work in behalf of the freedmen, were prompted by cultural rather than religious motives in directing attention to negro songs. They deplored the fact that circumstances made the collection almost wholly religious. Mr. Allen wrote: "I never fairly heard a secular song among the Port Royal freedmen, and never saw a musical instrument among them. The last violin, owned by a 'worldly man,' disappeared from Coffin's Point 'de year gun shoot at Bay Pint' (*i. e.*, November, 1861). In other parts of the South 'fiddle sings,' 'devil songs,' 'corn songs,' 'jig tunes' and what not, are common; all the world knows the banjo and the 'Jim Crow' songs of thirty years ago. We have succeeded in obtaining only a very few songs of this character. Our intercourse with the colored people has been chiefly through the work of the Freedmen's Commission, which deals with the serious and earnest side of the negro character"; and, discussing the "civilized" character of the songs which he prints, he says: "It is very likely that if we had found it possible to get at more of their secular music we should have come to another conclusion as to the proportion of the barbaric element." Then he makes room for a letter from "a gentleman from Delaware," who makes a number of shrewd observations, as thus:

We must look among their non-religious songs for the purest specimens of negro minstrelsy. It is remarkable that they have themselves transferred the best of these to the uses of their churches, I suppose on Mr. Wesley's principle that "it is not right that the devil should have all the good tunes." Their leaders and preachers have not found this change difficult to effect, or at least they have taken so little pains about it that one often detects the profane cropping out and revealing the origin of their most solemn "hymns" in spite of the best intentions of the poet and artist. Some of the best pure negro songs I have ever heard were those that used to be sung by the black stevedores, or perhaps the crews themselves, of the West India vessels, loading and unloading at the wharves in Philadelphia and Baltimore. I have stood for more than an hour, often, listening to them as they hoisted and lowered the hogsheads and boxes of their cargoes, one man taking the burden of the song (and the slack of the rope) and the others striking in with the chorus. They would sing in this way more than a dozen different songs in an hour, most of which might, indeed, be warranted to contain "nothing religious"—a few of them, "on the contrary, quite the reverse"—but generally rather innocent and proper in their language and strangely attractive in their music.

[34]

A generation ago songs of the character described here were still to be heard from the roustabouts of the Mississippi and Ohio rivers, and two of them, together with a paddle song dating back to the time of the Acadians, showing unique characteristics, will be discussed later.

M. Tiersot's generalizations on negro music, to which, it may be said, he denies all African attributes because the blacks have forgotten the language and customs of their ancestors, were based chiefly on reports of plantation life in which old French and Spanish influences were less potent than English. He recognizes the existence of a species of dance-song in which French influences have been predominantly formative, however, and discusses them in an interesting and instructive manner. They are the patois songs of the black creoles of Louisiana, concerning which I shall have something to say in due time. They are songs of sentiment and songs of satire—the latter characteristic, I believe, a relic of their African source. There is another, smaller, body of songs outside of the religious domain to which the spirituals give expression which would, I am convinced, have been of large value in proving the persistence of African idioms in exotic American songs if it had been possible to obtain a sufficient number of them to make a comparative study possible. Unfortunately this is not the case, and I very much question whether it will ever be done. The investigation has been postponed too long. The opportunity would have been incalculably greater half a century ago, when the subject was new. I made an effort to get some of these songs thirty-five years or so ago, when much more of this music was in existence than now, and, though I had the help of so enthusiastic a folklorist as the late Lafcadio Hearn, they eluded me. A few specimens came into my hands, but they proved to be of no musical value, chiefly because it was obvious that they had not been correctly transcribed.

The songs in question are those which were consorted with the mysterious voodoo rites practised by the blacks, who clung to a species of snake-worship which had been brought over from Africa. The preservation of relics of this superstitious worship until a comparatively late date was no doubt due to the negroes who had been brought into American territory long after the abolition of the slave trade. At the outbreak of the War of the Rebellion the number of these people was by no means inconsiderable. Though the slave trade was abolished by the United States in 1808 and those who followed it were declared pirates in 1820, negroes brought over from Africa were smuggled into the States by way of the Antilles for many years. It was not until 1861 that a trader was convicted under the law and hanged in New York. As late as 1888 Professor Edwards, describing the negro inhabitants of the Bahamas, who had already enjoyed freedom for more than fifty years, could write: "There lives yet in Green Turtle Cay one old negro, 'Unc' Yawk,' who, bowing his grizzled head, will tell you, 'Yah, I wa' fum Haf'ca.' "

It is well to remember facts like these when it is urged, as it is even by so good a musical folklorist as M. Tiersot, that African relics are not to be sought for in the music of the American negroes because they have forgotten the languages (not language) of their African ancestors. In the songs which have been heard by the few people who have left us accounts of the voodoo rites, African words are used, though their meaning has been lost. The phenomenon is not at all singular. Plato found the Egyptian priests using in their prayers, instead of words, the sacred vowels of their language, which they said had been taught their ancestors by Isis and Osiris. Buddhist monks in China, I have been told, still recite prayers in Sanskrit, though they do not understand a single word; small wonder, for nearly two thousand years have passed since Buddhism was introduced into China from India. The Gothic Christians at the time of the venerable Bede recited the Lord's Prayer in Greek. Is it difficult to understand what this means? Religion is a wonderful conservator. A greater sanctity attaches in worship to sounds than to words, for the first prayers were exclamations which came straight from the emotions—not words, but musical cries. It is for this reason that sacred music endures longer than articulate

speech. A veneration which is very much akin to superstition clings to both words and music in many organized
religious systems to-day. Would it be irreverent to account
on this ground for the attitude of the Pope and the Congregation of Rites toward the Gregorian Chant? Why is the
effort making to ignore the wise reforms of the sixteenth
century and revert to the forms of the tenth? Since it
is more than likely that the old dances and superstitious
rites of African peoples have left an impress upon the
music of their descendants in America, regard must be
had for these things, even though we must forgo such
an analytical study of the music as we should like to make.

In 1878, while Lafcadio Hearn and I were collaborating
in an effort to gather material for a study of creole music,
I sent him (he was then living in New Orleans) the words
of a song which I had got—I do not remember where—
for interpretation. In reply he wrote:

Your friend is right, no doubt, about the

"*Tig, tig, malaboin*
La chelema che tango
Redjoum!"

I asked my black nurse what it meant. She only laughed and shook her
head: "Mais c'est Voudoo, ça; je n'en sais rien!" "Well," said I, "don't you
know anything about Voudoo songs?" "Yes," she answered; "I know Voudoo
songs; but I can't tell you what they mean." And she broke out into the
wildest, weirdest ditty I ever heard. I tried to write down the words; but as
I did not know what they meant I had to write by sound alone, spelling the
words according to the French pronunciation.

He sent me the words and also the words of a creole
love-song, whose words ran like this: "Beautiful American,
I love thee! Beautiful American, I am going to Havana
to cut sugar-cane to give thee money. I am going to
Havana, friends, to cut sugar-cane, friends, to give thee
money, beautiful woman, Césaire! I love thee, beautiful
American!" He got a German amateur musician to write
down the music to both songs for him, but it was from his
singing that the transcription was made, and when it was
repeated to him he found it incorrect. Hearn was not
musical. "As I heard it sung the voodoo melody was
really weird, although simple," he wrote me afterward;
"there were such curious linkings of long notes to short
with microscopic ones. The other, 'Belle Américaine,'

seemed to me pretty, but G. has put only two notes where I heard five distinctly." The nurse who sang for him was Louise Roche, "an old black woman of real African blood, an ex-slave having many tales of terror, suspected of voodooism, etc."

Much later (it was in 1885), when I was contemplating a coöperation with Mr. George W. Cable in the articles which he published in the "Century Magazine" for February and April, 1886, on creole songs and dances, Hearn wrote:

I fear I know nothing about Creole music or Creole negroes. Yes, I have seen them dance; but they danced the Congo and sang a purely African song to the accompaniment of a drygoods box beaten with sticks or bones and a drum made by stretching a skin over a flour barrel. That sort of accompaniment and that sort of music you know all about; it is precisely similar to what a score of travellers have described. There are no harmonies—only a furious contretemps. As for the dance—in which the women do not take their feet off the ground—it is as lascivious as is possible. The men dance very differently, like savages, leaping in the air. I spoke of this spectacle in my short article in the "Century." . . . .

The Creole songs which I have heard sung in the city are Frenchy in construction, but possess a few African characteristics of method. The darker the singer, the more marked the oddities of intonation. Unfortunately, the most of those I have heard were quadroons or mulattoes. One black woman sang me a Voudoo song, which I got Cable to write—but I could not sing it as she sang it, so that the music is faulty. I suppose you have seen it already, as it forms part of the collection.

It was about this time (February, 1884, unless I am deceived by a postmark) that Hearn conceived the idea of a book on negro music, of which we were to be joint authors. He was to write "a long preface and occasional picturesque notes" to what he called my "learning and facts." He outlined what he would put in the preface: He would begin by treating of the negro's musical patriotism—"the strange history of the *griots*, who furnish so singular an example of musical prostitution, and who, though honored and petted on one way, are otherwise despised by their own people and refused rites of burial." Then he proposed to relate:

Something about the curious wanderings of these *griots* through the yellow desert northward into the Maghreb country, often a solitary wandering; their performances at Arab camps on the long journey, when the black slaves came out to listen and weep; then the hazardous voyage into Constantinople, where they play old Congo airs for the great black population of Stamboul, whom no laws or force can keep within doors when the sound of *griot* music is heard in the street. Then I would speak of how the blacks carry their music with them to Persia and even to mysterious Hadramant, where their voices are held in high esteem by Arab masters. Then I would touch upon the transplantation of negro melody to the Antilles and the two Americas, where its strangest black flowers are gathered by the alchemists of musical science and the perfume thereof extracted by magicians like Gottschalk. (How is that for a beginning?)

Having advanced thus far Hearn proposed to show a relation between physiology and negro music, and he put upon me the burden of finding out whether or not the negro's vocal cords were differently formed and "capable of longer vibrations" than those of white people. He had been led into this branch of the subject by the observation, which he found in some book, that the blood of the African black "has the highest human temperature known— equal to that of the swallow—though it loses that fire in America." I must have been lukewarm in the matter of the project which he outlined with great enthusiasm, despairing, as naturally a sobersided student of folk-music who believed in scientific methods would, of being able to make the physical data keep pace with so riotous an imagination as that of my fantastical friend. I did not even try to find a colored subject for the dissecting table or ask for a laryngoscopical examination of the vocal cords of the "Black Patti." His enthusiasm and method in our joint work are strikingly illustrated in another part of the same letter. As has been intimated, we were looking for unmistakable African relics in the creole songs of Louisiana:

Here is the only Creole song I know of with an African refrain *that is still sung*—don't show it to C., it is one of *our* treasures. (Pronounce "wenday," "makkiah.")

> Ouendé, ouendé, macaya!
> Mo pas barrassé, macaya!
> Ouendé, ouendé, macaya!
> Mo bois bon divin, macaya!
> Ouendé, ouendé, macaya!
> Mo mangé bon poulet, macaya!
> Ouendé, ouendé, macaya!
> Mo pas barrassé, macaya!
> Ouendé, ouendé, macaya!
> Macaya!

I wrote from the dictation of Louise Roche. She did not know the meaning of the refrain—her mother had taught her, and the mother had learned it from the grandmother. However, I found out the meaning, and asked her if she *now* remembered. She leaped in the air for joy—apparently. *Ouendai*, or *ouendé*, has a different meaning in the eastern Soudan; but in the Congo, or Fiot, dialect it means "to go," "to continue to," "to go on." I found the word in Jeannest's vocabulary. Then *macaya* I found in Turiault's "Étude sur la Language Créole de la Martinique": "ça veut dire manger tout le temps"—"excessivement." Therefore, here is our translation:

Go on! go on! *eat enormously!*
I ain't one bit ashamed—*eat outrageously!*
Go on! go on! *eat prodigiously!*
I drink good wine!—*eat ferociously!*
Go on! go on! *eat unceasingly!*—
I eat good chicken—gorging myself!
Go on! go on! etc.

How is this for a linguistic discovery? The music is almost precisely like the American river music—a chant, almost a recitative, until the end of the line is reached: then for your mocking music!

There is a hint of an African relic in the allusion to the recitative-like character of the feasting song, as we shall see when we come to inquire into the structure of African music.

For a description of the voodoo rites I draw, by permission, upon Mr. George W. Cable's article on "Creole Slave Songs," which appeared in "The Century Magazine" for April, 1886:

The dance and song entered into the negro worship. That worship was as dark and horrid as bestialized savagery could make the adoration of serpents. So revolting was it, and so morally hideous, that even in the West Indian French possessions a hundred years ago, with the slave trade in full blast, and the West Indian planter and slave what they were, the orgies of the voudoos were forbidden.

The Aradas, St. Méry tells us, introduced them from their homes beyond the Slave Coast, one of the most dreadfully benighted regions of all Africa. He makes the word vaudau. In Louisiana it is written voudou and voodoo and is often changed on the negro's lips to hoodoo. It is the name of an imaginary being of vast supernatural powers, residing in the form of a harmless snake. This spiritual influence, or potency, is the recognized antagonist and opposite of Obi, the great African manitou, or deity, whom the Congos vaguely generalize as Zombi. In Louisiana, as I have been told by that learned Creole scholar, the late Alexander Dimitry, Voodoo bore, as a title of greater solemnity, the additional name Maignan, and that even in the Calinda dance, which he had witnessed innumerable times, was sometimes heard at the height of its frenzy the invocation—

"Aïe! Aïe! Voudoo Maignan!"

The worship of Voodoo is paid to a snake kept in a box. The worshippers are not merely a sect, but in some rude, savage way, also an order. A man and woman, chosen from their own number to be the oracles of the serpent-deity, are called the king and queen. The queen is the more important of the two, and even in the present dilapidated state of the worship in Louisiana, where the king's office has almost or quite disappeared, the queen is still a person of great note. It (voodoo worship) long ago diminished in frequency to once a year, the chosen night always being the eve of St. John. For several years past the annual celebrations have been suspended; but in the summer of 1884 they were—let it be hoped only for the once—resumed. . . .

Now a new applicant for membership steps into the circle. There are a few trivial formalities and the voodoo dance begins. The postulant dances frantically in the middle of the ring, only pausing, from time to time, to receive heavy alcholic draughts in great haste and return more wildly to his leapings and writhings until he falls in convulsions. He is lifted, restored, and presently conducted to the altar, takes his oath, and by a ceremonial stroke from one of the sovereigns is admitted a full participant in the privileges and obligations of the devilish free masonry. But the dance goes on about the snake. The contortions of the upper part of the body, especially of the neck and shoulders, are such as to threaten to dislocate them. The queen shakes the box and tinkles the bells, the rum bottle gurgles, the chant alternates between king and chorus:

"Eh! Eh! Bomba honc, honc!
Canga bafio tay.
Canga moon day lay,
Canga do keelah,
Canga li!"

There are swoonings and ravings, nervous tremblings beyond control, incessant writhings and turnings, tearing of garments, even biting of the flesh—every imaginable invention of the devil.

CHAPTER IV

MODAL CHARACTERISTICS
OF THE SONGS

AN ANALYSIS OF HALF A THOUSAND NEGRO SONGS—
DIVISION AS TO MODES—OVERWHELMING PREVA-
LENCE OF MAJOR—PSYCHOLOGY OF THE PHENO-
MENON—MUSIC AS A STIMULUS TO WORK—
SONGS OF THE FIELDHANDS AND ROWERS.

To lay a foundation for a discussion of the idioms of the
folksongs created by the American negroes I have examined
527 negro songs found in six collections, five of which have
appeared in print. Of these five collections, four are
readily accessible to the student. The titles of the printed
collections are :

"Slave Songs of the United States," edited by William
Francis Allen, Charles Pickard Ware and Lucy McKim
Garrison; published by A. Simpson & Co., New York,
1867. This work, by far the most valuable and compen-
dious source, as it is the earliest, is out of print and difficult
to obtain.

"The Story of the Jubilee Singers, with Their Songs,"
by J. B. T. Marsh. Published by Houghton, Osgood & Co.,
Boston, 1880. This is a revised edition of two earlier
publications, the music arranged by Theodore F. Seward
and George L. White, of which the first was printed by
Bigelow & Main, New York, in 1872.

"Religious Folk Songs of the Negroes as Sung on the
Plantations," arranged by the musical directors of the
Hampton Normal and Agricultural Institute from the
original edition of Thomas P. Fenner. Published by the
Institute Press, Hampton, Va., 1909. The original edition,
entitled "Cabin and Plantation Songs as Sung by the
Hampton Students," was published in 1874; an enlarged
edition by Thomas P. Fenner and Frederic G. Rathbun,
by G. P. Putnam's Sons, New York, in 1891.

[42]

MODAL CHARACTERISTICS OF THE SONGS

"Bahama Songs and Stories. A Contribution to Folk-Lore," by Charles L. Edwards, Ph. D. Boston and New York, published for the American Folk-Lore Society by Houghton, Mifflin & Co., 1895.

"Calhoun Plantation Songs," collected and edited by Emily Hallowell; first edition, 1901; second edition, 1907; Boston, C. W. Thompson & Co.

These books, as well as the author's private collection, have been drawn on not so much to show the beauty and wealth of negro folksong as to illustrate its varied characteristics. An analysis of the 527 songs in respect of the intervallic structure of their melodies is set forth in the following table:

Ordinary major	331
Ordinary minor	62
Mixed and vague	23
Pentatonic	111
Major with flatted seventh	20
Major without seventh	78
Major without fourth	45
Minor with raised sixth	8
Minor without sixth	34
Minor with raised seventh (leading-tone)	19

"Almost all their songs were religious in their tone, however quaint their expression, and were in a minor key, both as to words and music," wrote Colonel Higginson, in "The Atlantic Monthly."—"They that walked in darkness sang songs in the olden days—sorrow songs—for they were weary at heart. . . . They (the songs) are the music of an unhappy people, of the children of disappointment; and they tell of death and suffering and unvoiced longing toward a truer world, of misty wanderings and hidden ways," says Dr. Du Bois, in "The Souls of Black Folk."—"A tinge of sadness pervades all the melodies, which bear as little resemblance to the popular Ethiopian melodies of the day as twilight to noonday," wrote Mr. Spaulding, in "The Continental Monthly." Mr. Allen, in his preface to "Slave Songs," avoids musical terminology as much as possible, and has nothing to say about the modes of the melodies which he records, though his description of the manner of singing and some of the peculiarities of intonation, in which I recognize characteristic idioms of the music, is so lucid as to enable a scientific student to form definite conclusions on technical points with ease. Colonel Higginson evidently did not intend that the word "minor" should have any other than its conventional literary meaning, which makes it a synonym for melancholy. The musical terminology of explorers, as has been remarked, is not to be depended on, and little is to be learned from them as to the prevailing modal characteristics of the music of the many peoples of Africa. Hermann Soyaux, in his "Aus West-Afrika," says that the negroes of Sierra Leone always sing in minor. Friedrich Ratzel says that the Bongo negroes sometimes sing in minor. "Their style," says Richard F. Burton, in the "Lake Regions of Central Africa," "is the recitative broken by a full chorus, and they appear to affect the major rather than the interminable minor of the Asiatic." Carl Engel, in his "Introduction to the Study of National Music," gives it out as a generalization that most of the African melodies are major. Of the seven African melodies which Coleridge-Taylor utilized in "Twenty-four Negro Melodies," five are major, two minor. Of the 527 melodies analyzed in the above table, less than 12 per cent are minor, the remainder either major or pentatonic, with a slight infusion, negligible at this stage of the argument, of melodies in which the mode is unpronounced.

It is plain, therefore, either that the popular conception, which I have permitted to stand with a qualification, of the minor mode as a symbol of suffering, is at fault in respect of the folksongs of the American negroes, or that these songs are not so poignant an expression of the life of the black slaves as has been widely assumed. The question deserves looking into. As a matter of fact, musicians know that the major and minor modes are not unqualified expressions of pleasure and pain, gayety and gravity, happiness and sorrow. Funeral marches are never expressions of joy, yet great funeral marches have been written in the major mode—Handel's Dead March in "Saul" for instance—and some of the maddest scherzos are minor. It may be questioned, too, whether or not, as a matter of fact (the physiological and psychological explanation of which is not within the scope of this study), the life of the black slaves was, on the whole, so weighted with physical and spiritual suffering as necessarily to make its musical expression one of hopeless grief. Perhaps an innate lightness of heart and carelessness of disposition, carefully cultivated by the slaveholders for obvious reasons, had much to do with the circumstance that there are few utterances of profound sadness or despair found in the songs, but many of resilient hopefulness and cheerful endurance of present pain in contemplation of the rewards of rest and happiness hereafter. The two emotional poles in question are touched in the settings of the song "Nobody Knows."

Colonel Higginson seems to have sounded the keynote of the emotional stimulus of the songs when he spoke of their infinite pathos as a commentary on the lives of their creators: "Nothing but patience for this life—nothing but triumph in the next." This feeling was encouraged by the attitude, legal and personal, of the slave owners toward their human chattels. To let them acquire an education was dangerous, for, as a rule, insurrections were fomented by educated men; but to encourage them in their rude, emotional religious worship was not harmful and might be positively beneficial. Under such circumstances it was natural that the poetical expressions of their temporal state should run out in religious allegory, and here the utterance had to be predominantly cheerful in the very nature of the case. They could not sing of the New Jerusalem, toward which they were journeying, in tones of grief. The Biblical tales and imagery, which were all of the book which seized upon their imagination, also called for celebration in jubilant rather than lugubrious accents. The rolling of Jordan's waters, the sound of the last trump, the overwhelming of Pharaoh's hosts, the vision of Jacob's ladder, the building of the Ark, Daniel in the den of lions, Ezekiel's "wheel in the middle of a wheel," Elijah's chariot of fire, the breaking up of the universe—all these things and the lurid pictures of the Apocalypse, whether hymned with allegorical intent or as literal conceptions, asked for swelling proclamation. And all received it.

[45]

It is possible, of course, even likely, though the records are not convincing, that restrictions were placed upon the songs of the slaves, in which an explanation may be found for the general tone of cheer, not unmixed with pathos, which characterizes the music. There is a hint of this in a remark recorded by Mrs. Frances Anne Kemble in her "Journal of a Residence on a Georgian Plantation," namely: "I have heard that many of the masters and overseers on these plantations prohibit melancholy tunes or words and encourage nothing but cheerful music and senseless words, deprecating the effect of sadder strains upon the slaves, whose peculiar musical sensibility might be expected to make them especially excitable by any songs of a plaintive character and having reference to their particular hardships." Examples of such restrictive regulations are not unknown to history. The Swiss soldiery in the French army were prohibited from singing the melody of the "Ranz des Vaches" because it produced homesickness, and the Austrian government has several times forbidden the sale of the Rakoczy March and confiscated the music found in the shops in times of political disturbance in Hungary.

Had the folksongs of the American negro been conceived in sorrow and born in heaviness of heart by a people walking in darkness, they could not have been used indiscriminately, as they were, for spiritual comfort and physical stimulation. It is the testimony of the earliest collectors that they were so used. Though it cannot be said that the employment of music to lighten and quicken work and increase its efficiency was peculiar to the slave life of America, it is nevertheless worth noting that this use, like some of the idioms of the music itself, was a relic of the life of the negroes in their aboriginal home. James Augustus Grant, in his book "A Walk Across Africa," as cited by Wallaschek, says that his people when cleaning rice were always supported by singers, who accompanied the workers with clapping of hands and stamping of feet. George Francis Lyon, in his "Narrative of Travels in Northern Africa," says that at one place he heard the negro women singing a national song in chorus while pounding wheat, always in time with the music. "Mr. Reade observed," says Wallaschek, citing W. Winwood Reade's "The African Sketch Book,"[1] "that his people always began to sing when he compelled them to overcome their natural laziness and to continue rowing." Here the song, of course, had for its purpose the promotion of synchronism in movement, like the rhythm of the march all the world over.

It is immaterial whether the use of song as a stimulant to work was brought from Africa or was acquired in America; the significant fact is that wherever negro slavery existed on this continent there it was found. In his peculiarly fascinating book "Two Years in the French West Indies," Lafcadio Hearn says: "Formerly the work of cane-cutting resembled the march of an army—first advanced the cutlassers in line, naked to the waist; then the *amareuses*, the women who tied and carried, and behind these the *ka*, the drum, with a paid *crieur* or *crieuse*, to lead the song, and lastly the black *commandeur* for general." In his preface to Coleridge-Taylor's "Twenty-four Negro Melodies" Booker T. Washington says: "Wherever companies of negroes were working together, in the cotton fields and tobacco factories, on the levees and steamboats, on sugar plantations, and chiefly in the fervor of religious gatherings, these melodies sprang into life. Oftentimes in slavery, as to-day in certain parts of the South, some man or woman with an exceptional voice was paid to lead the singing, the idea being to increase the amount of labor by such singing." And thus speaks the writer of the article entitled "American Music" in "The American History and Encyclopædia of Music," published by Irving Squire: "Work on the plantations was often done to the accompaniment of songs, whose rhythmic swing acted as an incentive to steadier and better labor; especially was this true with the mowers at harvest. Charles Peabody tells of a leader in a band of slaves who was besought by his companions not to sing a certain song because it made them work too hard. Again, on the

[1] Vol. II, page 313.

boats plying between the West Indies and Baltimore and the Southern ports, which were manned by the blacks, song was used for the same purpose. Later, on the Southern river boats, the same method was utilized. These boat-songs usually were constructed of a single line followed by an unmeaning chorus, the solo being sung by one of the leaders and the rhythmic refrain repeated over and over by the workers."

There is nothing especially characteristic of slave life in such "water music" except its idiom. The sailorman's "chanty," I fancy, is universal in one form or another. The singular fact to be noted here is that the American negro's "spirituals" were also his working songs, and the significance which this circumstance has with relation to their mood and mode. The spirituals could not have been thus employed had they been lugubrious in tone or sluggish in movement. The paucity of secular working songs has already been commented on. Of songs referring to labor in the field the editors of "Slave Songs of the United States" were able to collect only two examples. Both of them are "corn songs," and the first is a mere fragment, the only words of which have been preserved being "Shock along, John." The second defied interpretation fifty years ago and is still incomprehensible:

> Five can't ketch me and ten can't hold me—
> Ho, round the corn, Sally!
> Here's your iggle-quarter and here's your count-aquils—
> Ho, round the corn, Sally!
> I can bank, 'ginny bank, 'ginny bank the weaver—
> Ho, round the corn, Sally!

"The same songs are used for rowing as for shouting," says Mr. Allen, and adds: "I know of only one pure boat song, the fine lyric, 'Michael, row the boat ashore'; and this I have no doubt is a real spiritual—it being the Archangel Michael that is addressed."

My analytical table shows that three-fifths of the songs which I have examined contain the peculiarly propulsive rhythmical snap, or catch, which has several times been described as the basis of "ragtime."

It is this rhythm which helps admirably to make a physical stimulus of the tunes, and it is noteworthy that it is equally effective in slow and fast time. Essentially, therefore, it has nothing to do with the secular dance, though it plays a large part in the "shout." Mr. Ware mentions twelve songs as among the most common rowing tunes, and says of them: "As I have written these tunes two measures are to be sung to each stroke, the first measure being accented by the beginning of the stroke, the second by the rattle of the oars in the rowlocks. On the passenger boat at the (Beaufort) ferry they rowed from sixteen to thirty strokes a minute; twenty-four was the average. Of the tunes I heard I should say that the most lively were 'Heaven bell a-ring,' 'Jine 'em,' 'Rain fall,' 'No man,' 'Bell da ring' and 'Can't stay behin' '; and that 'Lay this body down,' 'Religion so sweet' and 'Michael, row,' were used when the load was heavy or the tide was against us."

A few additonal comments seem to be justified by these songs. Of the twelve, only three contain references to a water passage of any sort. In "Praise member"[1] two lines run:

> Jordan's bank is a good old bank,
> And I hain't but one more river to cross.

In "Michael, row the boat ashore" the archangel's boat is darkly described as a "gospel boat" and also as a "music boat," but there is no connection betwen these epithets and the rest of the song. "Praise member" presented a riddle to the editors, which they might have solved had they reflected on the effect which its use as a rowing song may have had upon its text.

Mr. Ware gives the last verse as "O I wheel to de right and I wheel to de left"; Colonel Higginson contributes a variant reading, "There's a hill on my leff, an' he catch on my right" and adds the only and unsatisfactory explanation given to him: "Dat mean if you go on de leff you go to 'struction, and if you go on de right go to God for sure." Miss Charlotte L. Forten has another version, "I hop on my right an' I catch on my leff," and makes the shrewd observation that she supposes that "some peculiar motion

[1] No. 5 of "Slave Songs."

of the body formed the original accompaniment of the song, but has now fallen into disuse." If the rowing singer meant "hold" or "stop" or "back" on my right and catch on my left, even a novice at the oars would have understood the motion as a familiar one in steering.

This is interesting, I think, though outside of the particular line of argument for which I introduced the working songs of the slaves—namely, to explain their general cheerfulness. Just as interesting is a singular custom which Mr. Reuben Tomlinson mentions in connection with the enigmatic song beginning "Rain fall and wet Becca Lawton," which has a refrain, "Been back holy, I must come slowly, Oh! Brudder, cry holy!" In place of "Been back" there are as variants "Beat back," "Bent back" and "Rack back." When the song is used for rowing, Mr. Tomlinson says, "at the words 'Rack back holy' one rower reaches back and slaps the man behind him, who in turn does the same and so on." It is not impossible, or even improbable, that this form of the game which was played in my boyhood, called "Pass it along," was an African survival.

It may be, too, that there is another relic, an African superstition, in the song. Colonel Higginson heard it as "Rain fall and wet Becky Martin"; a variant of the first line of the song as printed in "Slave Songs" is "Sun shine and dry Becca Lawton." Colonel Higginson comments: "Who Becky Martin was, and why she should or should not be wet, and whether the dryness was a reward or a penalty, none could say. I got the impression that in either case the event was posthumous, and that there was some tradition of grass not growing over the grave of the sinner; but even this was vague, and all else vaguer." In their note on the song the editors of "Slave Songs" say: "Lieutenant-Colonel Trowbridge heard a story that *Peggy Norton* was an old prophetess who said that it would not do to be baptized except when it rained; if the Lord was pleased with those who had been 'in the wilderness', he would send rain." To go into the wilderness was to seek conversion from sin, to go to "the mourners' bench," as our Methodist brethren say. Mr. Tomlinson said that the song always ended with a laugh, and he concluded from this that the negroes themselves regarded it as mere nonsense.

Not much else are the words of two Mississippi River songs, which are printed herewith, the music of which, however, has elements of unique interest. "Oh, Rock Me, Julie," (see p. 52) and "I'm Gwine to Alabamy" (see p. 53), are singularly alike in structure, with their exclamatory cadenza. They are also alike in bearing a resemblance to the stereotyped formula of the music of the North American Indians, with its high beginning and the repetition of a melodic *motif* on lower degrees of the scale. But "Rock Me, Julie," is unique in being built on the whole-tone scale, which has caused so much comment since Debussy exploited it in artistic music.

There is nothing in either words or music necessarily to connect a "Cajan" boat-song in my manuscript collection (see page 54) with the folksongs of the negroes, but the song is intrinsically interesting as a relic of the Acadian period in Louisiana. It was written down for me from memory a generation ago by Mrs. Wulsin, mother of the late Lucien Wulsin, of Cincinnati, a descendant, I believe, of one of the old *couriers des bois*. It is a canoe, or paddling, song, and there is no trace of the creole patois in its text.

> Les marenquins nous piquent—
> Il faut pagayer;
> L'on ne passe sa vie
> Toujours en pagayant.
> Pagaie, pagaie, pagaie, mon enfant.

(The mosquitoes sting us; we must paddle. One's life is not all passed in paddling. Paddle, paddle, paddle, my boy.)

The lines in the second verse as they remained in Mrs. Wulsin's memory do not adjust themselves to the melody, but they, no doubt, preserve the sense of the old song:

> Toute la semaine
> L'on mange de la sacamité,
> Et le Dimanche pour se régaler
> L'on mange du gombo filé.
> Pagaie, etc.

(All the week we eat *sacamité*, and on Sundays, for good cheer, we eat *gombo filé*. Paddle, etc.)

Oh! Rock Me, Julie

Words and melody received by the author from Mr. George W. Cable. The arrangement made
for this work by H. T. Burleigh. The melody is based on the "whole-tone" scale,

I'm Gwine to Alabamy

Moderato

1. I'm gwine to Al - a - bamy, Oh!

For to see my mam-my, Oh!

2. She went from ole Virginny,
   And I'm her pickaninny.

3. She lives on the Tombigbee,
   I wish I had her wid me.

4. Now I'm a good big nigger,
   I reckon I won't git bigger.

5. But I'd like to see my mammy,
   Who lives in Alabamy.

"A very good specimen, so far as notes can give one," says the editor of "Slave Songs of the United States", "of the strange barbaric songs that one hears upon the Western Steamboats." The arrangement made for this work by H. T. Burleigh.

Acadian Boatmen's Song

Written down as a recollection of her childhood in New Orleans by Mrs. Wulsin, mother of the late Lucien Wulsin of Cincinnati, for the author. The arrangement made for this publication by H. T. Burleigh.

"Sacamité," Lafcadio Hearn wrote in my notebook, "is a favorite Creole (and, of course, Acadian) dish made of corn broken and boiled with milk into a sort of thick soup. I do not know the etymology of this word."

CHAPTER V

MUSIC AMONG THE AFRICANS

The Many and Varied Kinds of African Slaves—
Not All Negroes—Their Aptitude and Love for
Music—Knowledge and Use of Harmony—
Dahomans at Chicago—Rhythm and
Drumming—African Instruments

So much for modes and moods. The analytical table
in the last chapter showed several variations of both the
major and minor scales, and these variations must be
examined, for upon them, together with rhythmical and
structural characteristics, rest the idioms which have been
referred to as determining the right of the songs of the
American negroes to be called original. These idioms are
the crude material which the slaves brought with them from
their African homes. This, at least, is the conviction of
this writer, and the contention which he hopes to establish
by a study of the intervallic and rhythmical peculiarities
of the songs and by tracing them to their primitive habitat.
Before then, for the sake of orderly argument, it may be
well briefly to inquire into the musical aptitude of the
Africans who created the idioms. Unfortunately, the
inquiry cannot be made as particular as might be desirable,
for want of specific evidence.

The slaves in the Southern States were an amalgamation
of peoples when the songs came into existence. Though
they are spoken of as negroes, there were many among them
who were not racially nigritians. The Slave Coast, from
which the majority of them were brought to America,
was the home of only a fraction of them. Many came from
the interior of the continent. There were some Malays
from Madagascar, some Moors from the northern portion
of the continent. Among the negroes of Africa the diver-
sities of tribe are so great that over a score of different
languages are spoken by them, to say nothing of dialects.

All was fish that came to the slaver's net. Among the Moors brought to America were men who professed the Mahometan religion and read and wrote Arabic. It is not impossible that to their influence in this country, or at any rate to Moorish influence upon the tribes which furnished the larger quota of American slaves, is due one of the aberrations from the diatonic scale which is indicated in the table—the presence of the characteristically Oriental interval called the augmented or superfluous second. Among the peoples who crowded the plantations were Meens, who were of the hue of the so-called red men of America— i. e., copper-colored. There were also Iboes, who had tattooed yellow skins. It does not seem to be possible now to recall all the names of the tributary tribes— Congos, Agwas, Popos, Cotolies, Feedas, Socos, Awassas, Aridas, Fonds, Nagos;—who knows now how they differed one from another, what were their peculiarities of language and music which may have affected the song which they helped to create in their second home? We must, perforce, generalize when discussing the native capacity for music of the Africans.

Sir Richard Francis Burton, in his book on West Africa, says of the music of the Kroomen that "it is monotonous to a degree, yet they delight in it, and often after a long and fatiguing day's march will ask permission to 'make play' and dance and sing till midnight. When hoeing the ground they do it to the sound of music; in fact, everything is cheered with a song. The traveller should never forget to carry a tom-tom or some similar instrument, which will shorten his journey by a fair quarter." In his "Lake Region of Central Africa" (page 291) Burton describes the natives of East Africa as "admirable timists and no mean tunists." Wallaschek (page 140), citing Moodie,[1] says: "Another still more striking example of the Hottentots' musical talent was related to Moodie by a German officer. When the latter happened to play that beautifully pathetic air of Gluck's, 'Che farò senza Euridice,' on his violin, he was surprised to observe that he was listened to by some

[1] "Ten Years in South Africa," by John W. D. Moodie, page 228.

Hottentot women with the deepest attention, and that some of them were even affected to tears. In a day or two afterward he heard his favorite melody, with accompaniments, all over the country wherever his wandering led him. At first it seems astonishing that there should be Hottentots apparently endowed with so great a musical gift; it is especially surprising to hear of their repeating the air with accompaniments, since the German officer was certainly not able to play both on his violin at the same time." Wallaschek then continues: "This statement, however, will no longer appear to us incredible if compared with similar examples in the accounts of some other travellers. Theophilus Hahn, who lived in Africa for fifteen years, tells us that his father, the missionary, used to play some hymns before the tribe of the Nama Hottentots to the accompaniment of a concertina. Some days afterward they would repeat the hymns *with the Dutch words,* which they could not understand. Hahn says: "They drawl the grave songs of the hymns, such as 'O Haupt voll Blut und Wunden,' 'Ein Lämmlein geht und trägt die Schuld,' with the same ardor as 'O du mein lieber Augustin,'[1] 'My Heart's in the Highlands' or 'Long, Long Ago.'"

This imitative capacity of the negroes frequently spoken of by travellers is amusingly described by Albert Friedenthal in his book, "Musik, Tanz und Dichtung bei den Kreolen Amerikas." One day in October, 1898, he was engaged in writing while sitting on his veranda at Lourenço Marques, on the east coast of Africa. Myriads of grasshoppers were devasting the country, and every negro far and near was pounding on something to drive the pests away. The noise became unendurable, and Friedenthal grabbed a tin plate and spoon from the hands of the first negro he reached and cried: "If you must make a noise, do it at least in this way!"—and he drummed out the rhythmical motive of the Nibelungs from Wagner's tetralogy. He repeated the figure two or three times. "Already the negroes in my garden imitated it; then, amused by it, those in the neighborhood took it up, and soon one

[1] The old German *Ländler,* "O du lieber Augustin," is meant.

could hear the Nibelung rhythm by the hour all over Delagoa Bay."

This author makes several allusions to the innate fondness of the negro for music and the influence which he has exerted upon the art of the descendants of the Spaniards in North and South America. On page 38 he writes:

But there is another race which has left its traces wherever it has gone—the African negroes. As has already been remarked, they have a share in the creation of one of the most extended forms, the Habanera. Their influence has been strongest wherever they have been most numerously represented—in the Antilles, on the shores of the Caribbean Sea and in Brazil. In places where the negro has never been—in the interior of Mexico, in Argentina, in Chili and the Cordilleran highlands—nothing of their influence is to be observed, except that in these countries the beautiful dance of the Habanera and numerous songs with the Habanera rhythm have effected an entrance.

On page 93:

From a musical point of view, the influence of the African on the West Indian Creole has been of the greatest significance, for through their coöperation there arose a dance-form—the Habanera—which spread itself through Romanic America. The essential thing in pure negro music, as is known, is to be sought in rhythm. The melodic phrases of the negroes consist of endless repetitions of short series of notes, so that we can scarcely speak of them as melodies in our sense of the word. On the other hand, no European shall escape the impression which these rhythms make. They literally bore themselves into the consciousness of the listener, irresistible and penetrating to the verge of torture.

On the same page again:

Whoever knows the enthusiastic love, I might almost say the fanaticism, of the negro for music can easily imagine the impression which the music of the Spaniards, especially that of the Creoles, made upon them. It can easily be proved how much they profited by the music of the Europeans, how gradually the sense of melody was richly developed in them, and how they acquired and made their own the whole nature of this art without surrendering their peculiarity of rhythm. This Europeanized negro music developed to its greatest florescence in the south of the United States.

Friedenthal mentions a number of musicians who attained celebrity, all of them of either pure or mixed African descent. They are José White, Brindis de Salas, Albertini, Gigueiroa and Adelelmo, violinists; Jimenez, pianist, and Coleridge-Taylor, composer. Of Adelelmo he says that though he was never heard outside of Brazil he was "an eminent virtuoso and refined composer; and, to judge by his surname (do Nascimento), probably the son of a former slave."

Wallaschek formulates his conclusion touching African music, after considering the testimony of travellers, as follows:

The general character of African music, then, is the preference for rhythm over melody (when this is not the sole consideration); the union of song and dance; the simplicity, not to say humbleness, of the subjects chosen; the great imitative talent in connection with the music and the physical excitement from which it arises and to which it appears appropriate.

In this characterization he might have included at least a rudimentary knowledge of, or feeling for, harmony. There is evidence of a harmonic sense in the American songs themselves, though the testimony of the original collectors does not make it clear that the slaves sang the characteristic refrains of their songs in parts. On this point something will have to be said presently; but the evidence of African harmony is summarized by Wallaschek himself in these words:

Kolbe at the beginning of the eighteenth century heard Hottentots playing their gom-goms in harmony. "They also sang the notes of the common chord down to the lower octave, each one beginning with the phrase whenever the former one had already come to the second or third tone, thus producing a harmonious effect."[1] Burchell describes the harmonious singing of the Bachapin boys: Sometimes one of them led the band and the rest joined in at different intervals and, guided only by the ear, attuned their voices in correct harmony. The elder boys, whose voices were of a lower pitch, sang the bass, while the younger produced in their turn the higher tones of the treble.[2] The Bechuanas also sing in harmony. The melody of their songs is simple enough, consisting chiefly of ascending and descending by thirds, while the singers have a sufficient appreciation of harmony to sing in two parts.[3] Moodie tells us that he very often heard the Hottentot servant girls singing in two parts; they even sang European tunes which were quite new to them with the accompaniment of a second of their own.[4] The same is said by Soyaux of the negro girls of Sierra Leone.[5]

Examples of harmony in the music of the Ashantees and Fantees, from Bowditch's "Mission from Cape Coast Castle to Ashantee," may be seen in the examples of African music printed in this chapter (pp. 61-62). That the Dahomans, who are near neighbors of the people visited by Bowditch, also employ harmony I can testify from observations made in the Dahoman village at the World's Columbian Exhibition held in Chicago in 1893. There I listened repeatedly during several days to the singing of a Dahoman

[1] Peter Kolbe, "Caput Bonae Spei Hodiernum," Nuremburg, 1719; page 528.

[2] W. T. Burchell, "Travels in the Interior of Southern Africa," London, 1822-'24; Vol. II, page 438.

[3] Ibid.

[4] Op. cit. II, 227.

[5] Hermann Soyaux, "Aus West-Afrika," Leipsic, 1879; II, 174.

African Music

No. 1. Drum Call from West Africa

No. 2. Tuning of a Zanze from South Africa

No. 3. Melody from the Ba-Ronga District

No. 4. A Melody of the Hottentots

No. 5. A Melody of the Kaffirs

No. 6. A War-Dance of the Dahomans

No. 7. Ashantee Air

No.8. Fantee Air

No.9. A Fantee Dirge

Specimens of African Music disclosing Elements Found in the Songs of the Negro Slaves in America.

No.1. A drum call from West Africa, utilized by Coleridge-Taylor in "Twenty-four Negro Melodies transcribed for the Piano" (Boston, Oliver Ditson Co.). The specimen exhibits the rhythmical "snap" or "catch", an exaggerated use of which has produced "rag-time"; also the fact that African drums are sometimes tuned.— No. 2. The tones given out by a *zanze* of the Zulus in the posession of the author; shows the pentatonic scale with two notes strange to the system at the end.— No.3. A pentatonic melody from "Les Chants et les Contes des Ba-Ronga", by Henri Junod, utilized by Coleridge-Taylor, who remarked of it that it was "certainly not unworthy of any composer— from Beethoven downwards".—No.4. A melody of the Hottentots, quoted by Engel in his "Introduction to the Study of National Music". It is in the major mode with the fourth of the scale omitted. The all-pervasive "snap" is present, as it is in– No.5. A Kaffir melody, also quoted by Engel; in the major mode (D) without the leading-tone.— No.6. Music of a dance of the Dahomans heard at the Columbian Exhibition in Chicago in 1893, illustrating the employment of the flat seventh and cross-rhythms between singers and drummers.— No.7. According to Bowdich ("Mission from Cape Coast Castle to Ashantee", London, 1819), the oldest air in his collection. Bowdich says: "I could trace it through four generations, but the answer made to my enquiries will give the best idea of its antiquity: 'It was made when the country was made'." It was played on the *sanko*, a rude guitar. It demonstrates the use of thirds.– No.8. A Fantee air from Bowdich's "Mission, etc.", showing thirds, fifths and the "snap".– No.9. A Fantee dirge for flutes and instruments of percussion. Also from Bowdich, who says: "In venturing the intervening and concluding bass-chord, I merely attempt to describe the castanets, gong-gongs, drums, etc., bursting in after the soft and mellow tones of the flutes; as if the ear was not to retain a vibration of the sweeter melody."

Round about the Mountain

A funeral hymn from Boyle Co., Kentucky, taken from the singing of a former slave by Miss Mildred J. Hill, for the author. Arranged by Arthur Mees. Miss Hill remarked on it: "Don't let this get to going in your mind, for it will give you no peace. It is worse than the 'A pink trip slip'. It seems quite high, but is the pitch in which it was sung."

minstrel who was certainly the gentlest and least assertive person in the village, if not in the entire fair. All day long he sat beside his little hut, a spear thrust in the ground by his side, and sang little descending melodies in a faint high voice, which reminded me of Dr. George Schweinfurth's description in his "Heart of Africa" of the minstrels of the Niam-Niam who, he said, are "as sparing of their voices as a worn-out prima donna," and whose minstrelsy might be said to have the "character of a lover's whisper." To his gentle singing he strummed an unvarying accompaniment upon a tiny harp. This instrument, primitive in construction (like the ancient Egyptian harps it lacked a pole to resist the tension of the strings), was yet considerably developed from an artistic point of view. It was about two and a half feet high and had eight strings accurately tuned according to the diatonic major system, but omitting the fourth tone. With his right hand he played over and over again a descending passage of dotted crochets and quavers in thirds; with his left hand he syncopated ingeniously on the highest two strings.

A more striking demonstration of the musical capacity of the Dahomans was made in the war-dances which they performed several times every forenoon and afternoon. These dances were accompanied by choral song and the rhythmical and harmonious beating of drums and bells, the song being in unison. The harmony was a tonic major triad broken up rhythmically in a most intricate and amazingly ingenious manner. The instruments were tuned with excellent justness. The fundamental tone came from a drum made of a hollowed log about three feet long with a single head, played by one who seemed to be the leader of the band, though there was no giving of signals. This drum was beaten with the palms of the hands. A variety of smaller drums, some with one, some with two heads, were beaten variously with sticks and fingers. The bells, four in number, were of iron and were held mouth upward and struck with sticks. The players showed the most remarkable rhythmical sense and skill that ever came under my notice. Berlioz in his supremest effort with his army of drummers produced nothing to compare in artistic interest with the harmonious drumming of these savages. The fundamental effect was a combination of double and triple time, the former kept by the singers, the latter by the drummers, but it is impossible to convey the idea of the wealth of detail achieved by the drummers by means of exchange of the rhythms, syncopation of both simultaneously, and dynamic devices. Only by making a score of the music could this have been done. I attempted to make such a score by enlisting the help of the late John C. Fillmore, experienced in Indian music, but we were thwarted by the players who, evidently divining our purpose when we took out our notebooks, mischievously changed their manner of playing as soon as we touched pencil to paper. I was forced to the conclusion that in their command of the element, which in the musical art of the ancient Greeks stood higher than either melody or harmony, the best composers of to-day were the veriest tyros compared with these black savages.

It would be easy to fill pages with travellers' notes on the drum-playing and dancing of the African tribes to illustrate their marvellous command of rhythm. I content myself with a few illustrative examples. African drums are of many varieties, from the enormous war drums, for which trunks of large trees provide the body and wild beasts the membranes which are belabored with clubs, down to the small vase-shaped instruments played with the fingers. The Ashantees used their large drums to make an horrific din to accompany human sacrifices, and large drums, too, are used for signalling at great distances. The most refined effects of the modern tympanist seem to be put in the shade by the devices used by African drummers in varying the sound of their instruments so as to make them convey meanings, not by conventional time-formulas but by actual imitation of words. Wallaschek[1] says:

"Peculiar to Africa is the custom of using drums as a means of communication from great distances. There are two distinctly different kinds of this drum language,

[1] Page 112.

as is shown in an example by Mr. Schauenburg. [1] He saw at Kujar a negro beating the drum with the right hand and varying the tone by pressing his left on the skin, so as to imitate the sound of the Mandingo words. During the wrestling match it sounded 'Amuta, amuta' (attack); during the dance 'ali bae si,' and all the participants understood it. [2] . . . . Sir A. C. Moloney observed this system of language among the Yorubas. . . and says it is an imitation of the human voice by the drum. To understand it one has to know 'the accents of pronunciation in the vernacular and to become capable of recognizing the different and corresponding note of the drum.' "

The art of making the drum talk is still known in the Antilles. In "Two Years in the French West Indies," [3] Lafcadio Hearn says:

The old African dances, the Caleinda and the Bélé (which latter is accompanied by chanted improvization), are danced on Sundays to the sound of the drum on almost every plantation in the land. The drum, indeed, is an instrument to which the countryfolk are so much attached that they swear by it, *Tambou!* being the oath uttered upon all ordinary occasions of surprise or vexation. But the instrument is quite as often called *ka* because made out of a quarter-barrel, or *quart*, in the patois *ka*. Both ends of the barrel having been removed, a wet hide, well wrapped about a couple of hoops, is driven on, and in drying the stretched skin obtains still further tension. The other end of the ka is always left open. Across the face of the skin a string is tightly stretched, to which are attached, at intervals of about an inch apart, very thin fragments of bamboo or cut feather stems. These lend a certain vibration to the tones.

In the time of Père Labat the negro drums had a somewhat different form. There were then two kinds of drums—a big tamtam and a little one, which used to be played together. Both consisted of skins tightly stretched over one end of a cylinder, or a section of a hollow tree-trunk. The larger was from three to four feet long, with a diameter of from 15 to 16 inches; the smaller, *Baboula*, was of the same length, but only eight or nine inches in diameter.

The skilful player (*bel tambouyé*), straddles his ka stripped to the waist, and plays upon it with the finger-tips of both hands simultaneously, taking care that the vibrating string occupies a horizontal position. Occasionally the heel of the naked foot is pressed lightly or vigorously against the skin so as to produce changes of tone. This is called "giving heel" to the drum— *bailly talon*. Meanwhile a boy keeps striking the drum at the uncovered end with a stick, so as to produce a dry, clattering accompaniment. The sound of the drum itself, well played, has a wild power that makes and masters all the excitement of the dance—a complicated double roll, with a peculiar

[1] Eduard Schauenburg, "Reisen in Central-Afrika," etc. Lahr, 1859, I, 93.

[2] Sir Alfred Moloney, "Notes on Yoruba and the Colony and Protectorate of Lagos," in The Proceedings of the Royal Geographical Society, New Series, XII, 596.

[3] Harper & Bros.; 1890.

billowy rising and falling. The creole onomatopes, *b'lip-b'lip-b'lip-b'lip*, do not fully render the roll; for each stands really for a series of sounds too rapidly flipped out to be imitated by articulate speech. The tapping of a ka can be heard at surprising distances; and experienced players often play for hours at a time without exhibiting wearisomeness, or in the least diminishing the volume of sound produced.

It seems that there are many ways of playing—different measures familiar to all these colored people, but not easily distinguished by anybody else; and there are great matches sometimes between celebrated *tambouyé*. The same *commandé* whose portrait I took while playing told me that he once figured in a contest of this kind, his rival being a drummer from the neighboring burgh of Marigot. . . .

"*Aie, aie, aie! mon chè—y fai tambou-a pàlé!*" said the *commandé*, describing the execution of his antagonist; "my dear, he just made that drum talk! I thought I was going to be beaten for sure; I was trembling all the time— *aie, yaïe, yaïe!* Then he got off that ka. I mounted it; I thought a moment; then I struck up the 'River-of-the-Lizard'—*mais, mon chè, yon larivié-Léza toutt pi!* such a 'River-of-the-Lizard,' ah! just perfectly pure! I gave heel to that ka;—I worried that ka; I made it mad; I made it crazy; I made it talk; I won!"

In Unyanebe, James Augustus Grant says, the large drum is played by the leader, while a youth apparently rattled a roll like the boy in Hearn's description. In my notebook I find a postcard, written by Hearn from New Orleans thirty years ago, which indicates that the manner of drumming described by Grant and also in the above excerpt was also common in Louisiana. Hearn writes: "The Voudoo, Congo and Caleinda dances had for orchestra the empty wooden box or barrel drum, the former making a dry, rapid rattle like castanets. The man sat astride the drum." Max Buchner[1] says that the drummer in Kamerun does not beat the time, but a continuous roll, the time being marked by the songs of the spectators. An example of the harmonious drumming such as I heard in the Dahoman village is mentioned by Hermann Wissmann in his book "Unter deutscher Flagge durch Afrika,"[2] who says that "when the chief of the Bashilange received the European visitors he was accompanied in his movements by a great drum with a splendid bass tone. When he declared friendship four well-tuned drums began to play, while the assembly sang a melody of seven tones, repeating it several times."[3]

The musical instruments used in Africa do not call for extended study or description here, since their structure

[1] "Kamerun," Leipsic, 1887, page 29.
[2] Berlin, 1889, page 72.
[3] Wallaschek, page 115.

has had nothing to do with influencing the forms of Afro-American folksong. The drum has received such extended attention only because it plays so predominant a rôle in the music of America as well as Africa. As the rhythmical figure which is characteristic of the Habanera (which dance Friedenthal asserts is indubitably of African origin) dominates the dance-melodies of Spanish America, so the "snap" which I have found in 315 of the 527 melodies analyzed, in its degenerate form of "ragtime" now dominates the careless music of two great countries—the United States and England.

Two instruments which would have been of incalculable value in determining the prevalent intervallic systems of African music, had the travellers who have described them been musically scientific enough to tell us how they were tuned, are the marimba and the zanze, both of which are found widely distributed over the Dark Continent. In these instruments the tone-producing agency is fixed when they are made and remains unalterable. The marimba, which has become a national instrument in Mexico, is an instrument of the xylophone type, the tones of which are struck out of sonorous bars of wood and intensified by means of dry calabashes of various sizes hung under the bars. The accounts of this instrument given by travellers do not justify an attempt to record its tunings. The zanze is a small sound-box, sometimes reinforced by a calabash or a block of wood hollowed out in the form of a round gourd, to the upper side of which, over a bridge, are tightly affixed a series of wooden or metal tongues of different lengths. The tongues are snapped with the thumbs, the principle involved being that of the familar music-box, and give out a most agreeable sound. I find no record in the accounts of travellers as to any systematic tuning of the instrument, but a specimen from Zululand in my possession is accurately tuned to the notes of the pentatonic scale, with the addition of two erratic tones side by side in the middle of the instrument—a fact which invites speculation.

In the table showing the results of an analysis of 527 songs, seven variations from the normal, or conventional, diatonic major and minor scales were recorded, besides the songs which were set down as of mixed or vague tonality. They were (1) the major scale, with the seventh depressed a semitone, *i.e.*, flatted; (2) the major scale, without the seventh or leading-tone; (3) the major scale, without the fourth; (4) the major scale, without either seventh of fourth (the pentatonic scale); (5) the minor scale, with a raised or major sixth; (6) the minor scale, without the sixth, and (7) the minor scale, with the raised seventh— the so-called harmonic minor. Their variations or aberrations shall occupy our attention in the next chapter. For the majority of them I have found prototypes in African music, as appears from the specimens printed in this chapter.

CHAPTER VI

VARIATIONS FROM THE MAJOR SCALE

Peculiarities of Negro Singing—Vagueness of Pitch in Certain Intervals—Fractional Tones in Primitive Music—The Pentatonic Scale—The Flat Seventh—Harmonization of Negro Melodies

Of the 527 songs examined I have set down in my table 331 as being in the major mode. To these, as emphasizing the essentially energetic and contented character of Afro-American music, notwithstanding that it is the fruit of slavery, must be added 111 which are pentatonic. Of the 331 major songs twenty, or a trifle more than one-sixteenth, have a flat seventh; seventy-eight—that is, one fourth—have no seventh, and forty-five, or nearly one-seventh, have no fourth. Fourth and seventh are the tones which are lacking in the pentatonic scale, and the songs without one or the other of them approach the pentatonic songs in what may be called their psychological effect. These are the only variations of the major scale which can be set down as characteristic of the songs. In the case of the songs in the minor mode, eight, a fraction under one-eighth, have a major sixth; over one-half have no sixth at all, and over one-third have the leading-tone (major seventh), which is not an element of the minor scale proper, but with the major sixth has been admitted through the use of accidentals to what musicians call the harmonic minor scale. In the case of twenty-three songs I have set down the mode as mixed or vague, because the scales do not conform to either the major or minor system, but, in part, to both, or have elements which are obviously sporadic.

It is necessary for a correct understanding of the nature of negro songs that the testimony of the collectors touching some of these aberrant intervals be heard. As I have set them down, the flat seventh in the major and major sixth in the minor are more or less approximations to the tones as they are sung; but the circumstances justify the classifications which I have made. In my own defence, though it may not be necessary to make one, I may say that here I am entirely dependent upon the evidence adduced by others; I did not hear the songs sung in slavery, nor did I come in closer touch with the generation which made them generally known than many of my readers who heard the Jubilee Singers of Fisk University on their first concert tour. It was their singing which interested me in the subject, and it was forty years ago that I began my observations, which I was not permitted to extend personally into the regions where research should have been made, and where I vainly tried to have it made through other agencies.

"It is difficult," said Miss McKim,[1] "to express the entire character of these negro ballads by mere musical notes and signs. The odd turns made in the throat and the curious rhythmic effect produced by single voices chiming in at different irregular intervals seem almost as impossible to place on the score as the singing of birds or the tones of an æolian harp."

"Another obstacle to its rendering is the fact that tones are frequently employed which we have no musical characters to represent. Such, for example, is that which I have indicated as nearly as possible by the flat seventh in 'Great Camp Meetin', 'Hard Trials,' and others," says Thomas P. Fenner, in the preface to "Cabin and Plantation Songs," and he continues: "These tones are variable in pitch, ranging through an entire interval on different occasions, according to the inspiration of the singer. They are rarely discordant, and even add a charm to the performance." Miss Emily Hallowell's "Calhoun Plantation Songs" bear evidence of having been more carefully noted than the Fisk or Hampton collections, though made at a much later date. In her preface Miss Hallowell says: "I have tried

[1] "Slave Songs," page 6.

to write them down just as they were sung, retaining all the peculiarities of rhythm, melody, harmony and text; but those who have heard these or other like songs sung by the colored people of the South will realize that it is impossible to more than suggest their beauty and charm; they depend so largely upon the quality of voice, the unerring sense of rhythm and the quaint religious spirit peculiar to the colored people who have spent their lives on Alabama cotton plantations, untouched by civilization." Miss Mildred J. Hill, of Louisville, who gathered for me some of the most striking songs in my collection from the singing of an old woman who had been a slave in Boyle County, Ky., was careful to note all deviations from just intonation, and from her songs I came to the conclusion that the negroes were prone to intervallic aberrations, not only in the case of the seventh, but also in the third. This is a common phenomenon in folk-music. It was the observation of the composer Spohr that rural people intone the third rather sharp, the fourth still sharper, and the seventh rather flat. Vagaries of this kind emphasize the fact that the diatonic scale—the tempered scale, at any rate— as used in artistic music is a scientific evolution, and not altogether a product of nature, as some persons assume, who in consequence attribute the slightest fractional variation from its tones to exquisite appreciation of tonal differences.

The speculations on this point in which some professed students of the music of the North American Indians have indulged have reached a degree of absurdity almost laughable. In one case changes of pitch, which were most obviously the result of differences of speed in the revolution of the cylinder of the phonograph used in the collection of Zuñi songs, were gravely declared to be evidence of a musical sense which could not be satisfied with the semitones of civilized musicians. The melodies had been recorded by treadle power and transmitted for notation by electric. To prove the valuelessness of music thus obtained I experimented with a pitch-pipe and a phonograph, and by varying the speed of the revolutions of the cylinder in making the record easily ran the pitch of my C up and down an octave like the voice of a siren. Why savages who have never developed a musical or any other art should be supposed to have more refined æsthetic sensibilities than the peoples who have cultivated music for centuries, passes my poor powers of understanding.

But the contemplation of savage life seems to have a tendency to make the imagination (especially that of sympathetic people) slip its moorings. My own experience with Indian music has convinced me that the red man is markedly unmusical. That appears to me to be amply proved by the paucity of melody in the songs of the Indians, their adherence to a stereotyped intervallic formula, regardless of the use to which the song is put, and their lack of agreement in pitch when singing. To the Indian music is chiefly an element of ritual; its practice is obligatory, and it is not *per se* an expression of beauty for beauty's sake or an emotional utterance which a love for euphony has regulated and moulded into a thing of loveliness. It reaches its climax in the wild and monotonous chants which accompany their gambling games and their ghost-dances.

There is a significance which I cannot fathom in the circumstance that the tones which seem rebellious to the negro's sense of intervallic propriety are the fourth and seventh of the diatonic major series and the fourth, sixth and seventh of the minor. The omission of the fourth and seventh intervals of the major scale leaves the pentatonic series on which 111 of the 527 songs analyzed are built. The fact is an evidence of the strong inclination of the American negroes toward this scale, which is even more pervasive in their music than it is in the folksongs of Scotland, popularly looked upon as peculiarly the home of the pentatonic scale. On this imperfect scale the popular music of China, Japan and Siam rests; it is common, too, in the music of Ireland, and I have found many examples in the music of the American Indians and the peoples of Africa. The melody of the "Warrior's Song" in Coleridge-Taylor's fine book of pianoforte transcriptions entitled "Twenty-four Negro Melodies,"[1] is a

[1] Boston: Oliver Ditson Company.

pentatonic tune from the Ba-Ronga country, and Coleridge-Taylor says of it that its subject "is certainly not
unworthy of any composer—from Beethoven downward.
It is at once simple, strong and noble, and probably stands
higher than any other example of purely 'savage' music in
these respects." Except that it lent itself so admirably
to artistic treatment, I cannot see why this melody should
have been singled out by Mr. Coleridge-Taylor for such
extraordinary praise; many of the American slave songs
are equally simple, strong and noble and more beautiful.
Yet it is a specially welcome example because it comes
from Africa.

The temptation is strong to look upon the pentatonic
scale as the oldest, as it certainly is the most widespread
and the most serviceable, of intervallic systems. It is the
scale in which melody may be said to be naturally innate.
Play it at random on the black keys of the pianoforte,
and so you keep symmetry of period and rhythm in mind
you cannot help producing an agreeable melody; and it will
be pentatonic. (See "Nobody Knows de Trouble I've
Seen," page 75.)

The history of the pentatonic scale has baffled investi-
gators, for it is older than history. China has a musical
instrument called *hiuen*, the invention of which is said
(fantastically, no doubt) to date back to B. C. 2800. It
emits only the five tones of the pentatonic scale. Instruments with the same limitations and qualities have been
found among the remains of the lost civilizations of Mexico
and Peru, and are still in existence in Nubia and Abyssinia.
I have mentioned a Zulu *zanze* which is in my possession—
a little instrument so stoutly built that it is likely to survive
centuries. It has pentatonic tuning down to two middle
tongues, which emit strangely aberrant tones. The key is
D-flat. The tongues on one side emit the descending order,
D-flat, E-flat and B-flat; on the other, B-flat, F, D-flat and
A-flat. The instrument is played by plucking and snap-
ping the metal tongues with the thumbs; any two plucked
by a thumb simultaneously produce an agreeable con-
cord. Between the right and left rows of tongues lie

Nobody Knows de Trouble I've Seen

An example of a melody in the pentatonic scale (without the fourth and seventh degrees). From "Slave Songs of the United States," the arrangement for this work by H. T. Burleigh.

the two which give out the strange, wild notes A and B. How these tones were melodically introduced only a musician hearing the instrument played by a native could tell.

In an article on Scottish music in Grove's "Dictionary of Music and Musicians" Mr. Frank Kidson observes that "whether this pentatonic series was acquired through the use of a defective instrument, or from the melodic taste of a singer or player, must remain mere matter of conjecture." Scarcely, so far as its hypothetical instrumental origin is concerned. The first melodies were vocal, and among primitive peoples instruments are made for the music—not music for the instruments. Defects in instruments are the results of faulty adjustments of mechanical means to desired ends. Prehistoric whistles, with finger-holes to produce five tones only, were made so that melodies with five tones might be played on them. The melodies were not invented because the makers of the whistles neglected to make a larger number of finger-holes or to dispose them differently.

Many years ago the Rev. Dr. Wentworth, the editor of "The Ladies' Repository," a magazine published by the Methodist Episcopal Church, who had been a missionary in China, told me that he had observed that his congregation became singularly and unaccountably dissonant at certain places in every hymn-tune adopted from the Methodist hymnal. When I told him that the Chinese, while admitting the theoretical existence of the fourth and seventh intervals of the diatonic scale, eschewed them in practice, and asked him whether or not they had been the troublesome tones, he expressed the opinion that I had explained a fact which he had looked upon as inexplicable. Not having made the experiment myself, I could not say whether or not he was right; but it is certainly conceivable that centuries of habit might atrophy the musical faculty of a people so as to make the production of a tone as part of an intervallic system difficult and lead to its modification when occasion called for its introduction. In some such manner it is not unlikely that the flat seventh of the major scale in the music of the American negroes may be accounted for. This, however, is a mere hypothesis. Though not a common feature of the folksongs of other peoples, it does occur here. It is found in a Servian *kolo* dance printed by Engel in his "Introduction to the Study of National Music," and also in some Arabic tunes. Students of the old ecclesiastical modes recognize it as an element of the Mixolydian mode, with its intervals G, A, B, C, D, E and F-natural.

Whether the employment of the flat seventh is due to an innate harmonic sense on the part of its users, which sometimes discloses itself very markedly in an evident feeling for the subdominant relationship, or is a purely melodic factor (as in Gregorian music), is a question which I shall not undertake to determine. In the case of a very stirring hymn, "Dere's a Great Campmeetin' " (see page 78), the harmonic impulse seems to me most obvious, though there is no other song which I have found in which the flat seventh strikes the ear with such barbaric force as it does in this. Here the first section of the melody closes with a perfect cadence in the key of E-flat; the second section begins abruptly with an apparently unrelated shout on D-flat—"Gwine to mourn, and nebber tire"— which leads directly, as the effect shows, into the key of A-flat, the subdominant of E-flat. The transition has a singularly bright and enlivening effect and the return to the original key is easy and natural.

The specimen illustrating the use of the flat seventh given in the examples of African prototypes in the preceding chapter was noted at the Chicago World's Fair by Heinrich Zoellner, the German composer. I was never fortunate enough in my visits to the Dahoman Village to hear the dancers sing. Mr. Zoellner witnessed two choral dances and wrote down the vocal music, which he placed at my disposal. In the first dance the Dahomans sang a slow phrase of two measures in C major without the seventh over and over again, while the band drummed in double time and the dancers advanced and retreated without particular regard to the rhythm, some individuals indulging in fancy steps *ad lib.* Then there came a change

A Great Campmeetin'

From the Hampton collection,"Religious Folk-Songs of the Negro." A fine example of the effect produced by the flat seventh.

of tempo and rhythm, and also in the manner of singing and dancing. The drummers changed from double to compound-triple time, the singers separated into two choirs and sang the antiphonal *Allegro* phrase printed in the table of examples, and began to keep step with absolute precision.

In what key is this phrase? Not in C minor, as the prevalence of C, E-flat and G would seem to suggest at first sight; the A is too disturbing for that. But if one should conceive the phrase as being in F, the explanation is at hand. Then it will be seen that the phrase illustrates the use of the flat seventh. This E-flat is now felt as the essential element of the dominant seventh-chord of the subdominant key, B-flat. In "A Great Campmeetin' " the corresponding tone leads into this key as the song is sung and as it appears in the books; but it must be observed that the harmonization was made by Mr. Fenner, who has not told us to what extent he received hints from his singers. The Dahomans seemed satisfied to treat the E-flat as a grace-note and found gratification for their sense of repose in the F major triad suggested by the concluding C. When I consulted Mr. Arthur Mees, who gave particular attention to the ecclesiastical modes when a student of Weitzmann, in Berlin, as to his opinion on the subject under consideration, he wrote me: "The use of the flat seventh seems to be quite common to old melodies. Just such a one as you quote as being Dahoman I found in an attempted deciphering of Hebrew melodies from Hebrew accents. It is, I think, true that the dropping into the subdominant is a sort of relaxation of musical fancy (*Vorstellung*), while modulation into the dominant is a climbing up process, which can be accomplished by not less than two chords. (I mean two different roots.) I do not feel a modulation with the introduction of the low seventh, but a melodic peculiarity which is enforced and made piquant by the mental effort (unconscious) to retain the original tonality after the flat seventh has been heard." Mr. Mees added that he felt the scale of the phrase just as he felt the scale of the Mixolydian mode.

Weeping Mary

Arranged for men's voices by Arthur Mees, for the Mendelssohn Glee Club of New York. By permission.

VARIATIONS FROM THE MAJOR SCALE

Some time afterward Mr. Mees arranged several negro songs for men's voices and performed them at a concert of the Mendelssohn Glee Club of New York. One of them was "Weeping Mary," which is reproduced in this chapter. (See page 80.) This brought the topic of how the negro songs ought to and might be harmonized into discussion, and Mr. Mees wrote me:

It is a most interesting subject. The first question that arises in examining a tone-succession so strange to us is this: Did the people to whom a particular one is credited intuitively *feel* a harmonic substratum to the melodies they invented? So far as the negroes are concerned, I believe that the intuition of harmony was peculiar to them. I have spoken with many Southern people, and they all speak of the love of harmony that is peculiar to the negroes. If that is true, the altered tones they introduce in the scales on which their melodies are constructed have a harmonic significance, and the frequent introduction of a minor seventh would point to a tendency toward the subdominant, as you suggest. This would be true of melodies in the major mode only, for the seventh in the minor mode, according to Weitzmann and his followers, is the normal tone in the minor mode, and the large seventh the variant, introduced because of the requirement in modern music of the leading-tone to make the cadence authoritative. . . .

In "Weeping Mary," which in my arrangement is in G minor, the E natural is very interesting and produces a fine effect. It is the raised sixth in minor. Ziehn in his "Harmonielehre" quotes a striking example of the same progression from Beethoven.

Mr. Mees's letter has brought us around again to the subject of the use of harmony in the Afro-American folk-songs. In "Slave Songs of the United States" the tunes only are printed, and of their performance Mr. Allen said in his preface:

There is no singing in *parts*, as we understand it, and yet no two appear to be singing the same thing; the leading singer starts the words of each verse, often improvising, and the others, who "base" him, as it is called, strike in with the refrain, or even join in the solo when the words are familiar. When the "base" begins the leader often stops, leaving the rest of the words to be guessed at, or it may be they are taken up by one of the other singers. And the "basers" themselves seem to follow their own whims, beginning when they please and leaving off when they please, striking an octave above or below (in case they have pitched the tune too high), or hitting some other note that chords, so as to produce the effect of a marvellous complication and variety and yet with the most perfect time and rarely with any discord. And what makes it all the harder to unravel a thread of melody out of this strange network is that, like birds, they seem not infrequently to strike sounds that cannot be precisely represented by the gamut and abound in "slides from one note to another and turns and cadences not in articulated notes."

The peculiar style of singing described in the concluding words has been made familiar by several singers who have used the songs on the concert platform, particularly by Mrs.

Jeannette Robinson Murphy. In a personal letter to the writer, dated July 16, 1913, Miss Emily Hallowell says of her book:

I have always thought that the time would come when some student would find the "Calhoun Collection" of greater service than most of the other publications, for two reasons: As far as my ability allowed they were written precisely as they were sung, while in most collections they have been arranged for ordinary quartet singing; and as the people of Calhoun are so much more remote than in most localities, their singing in 1900 was almost exactly as it was before the war. . . . I got most of the songs from young people, too young to remember slavery, but I have heard many of them sung by the old people, and the melodies were the same, but the harmonies I have written were all taken from the pupils in the Calhoun school. The old people's harmonies seem to arise from each holding to their own version of the melodies or from limitation of compass.

I have cited instances of the employment of harmony in Africa. In my notebook I find an interesting example, which I obtained from Mr. George L. White, teacher and manager of the Jubilee Singers after their return from their memorable trip to Germany in 1877. It is a hymn which Dr. Wangemann heard sung, with great effect, as he testified, by a congregation of three hundred Kaffirs in a Presbyterian mission in Emgravali. Its composition was attributed to a Kaffir named U-Utrikana, the first member of his tribe to embrace Christianity, who became a sort of black Sankey and travelled all over his country as a singing evangelist. "He was honored as a prophet by his people," wrote Dr. Wangemann on the transcript of the hymn which he made from memory for Mr. White. What the words mean I do not know, but musically the song consists of two solos and refrains, the solos sung in unison, the refrains in full harmony, consisting of the tonic and dominant triads. As a rule, the songs of the Afro-Americans are so obviously built on a harmonic basis and show so plainly the influence of civilized music that I have no doubt the majority of them were sung in simple harmony— at least the refrains. The phrases containing the "wild notes," as I call them, were just as certainly sung in unison and are most effective when left without harmony, as is the rule (though I have made a few exceptions) in this collection.

CHAPTER VII

MINOR VARIATIONS
AND CHARACTERISTIC RHYTHMS

VAGARIES IN THE MINOR SCALE—THE SHARP SIXTH—
ORIENTALISM—THE "SCOTCH" SNAP—A NOTE ON
THE TANGO DANCE—EVEN AND UNEVEN MEAS-
URES—ADJUSTING WORDS AND MUSIC

The frequent aberrations from the major scale in the songs of the American negroes, which I have pointed out, serve effectually to disprove Wallaschek's contention that they are nothing more than imitations of European songs— "unmistakably arranged" or "ignorantly borrowed" from the national songs of European peoples. There is but one body of specifically national song with which the slave of the United States could by any possibility have become familiar—the Scottish, with its characteristic pentatonic scale and rhythmical snap; but the singing of Scottish ballads was not so general in the South that their peculiarities could become the common property of the field hands on the plantations. The negroes in the Antilles and South America were in a very different case. Reciprocal influences were stronger there, where social lines were more loosely drawn and where the races amalgamated to an extent which threatened the institution of slavery itself; but even there the impress of African music is unmistakable and indelible. Spanish melody has been imposed on African rhythm. In the United States the rhythmical element, though still dominant, has yielded measurably to the melodic, the dance having given way to religious worship, sensual bodily movement to emotional utterance.

The demonstration of independence of European influence is still more striking in the case of the minor songs and those of mixed or vague tonality. The variations from the minor scale which I have classified are those disclosing the major seventh (the leading-tone), the use of the major sixth and the absence of the sixth. Other aberrations are not pronounced enough to justify being set down as characteristic features.

There is no special significance in the prevalence of the leading-tone in minor melodies (it was found in nineteen songs out of sixty-two), beyond the evidence which it may offer of the influence of the European system in which the seventh step of the minor scale is arbitrarily raised a semitone for the sake of a satisfactory harmonic cadence. To avoid the abnormal interval of a second consisting of three semitones European theorists also raise the sixth, thus obtaining the conventional ascending minor scale— the melodic minor. It cannot be without significance that what I am prone to consider a primitive melodic sense seems to have led the negroes to rebel at this procedure. In thirty-four out of sixty-two minor melodies the troublesome sixth (the avoided fourth in the major mode) is omitted entirely, and in eight it is raised to a major interval without disturbing the seventh. The major sixth in the minor mode presents itself as an independent melodic element, the effect of which is most potently felt when it is left unharmonized—which is not the case in one of the illustrative examples which I present.[1] The minor tunes with the major sixth are thus without the leading-tone, and the physiological effect of the errant interval is even more striking than the flat seventh in the major tunes.

No one who heard Miss Jackson, the contralto of the original Fisk Jubilee choir, sing "You May Bury Me in the East,"[2] without accompaniment of any sort, is likely to have forgotten the clarion sound of her voice on the word "trumpet." This was the only song of its kind in the repertory of the Jubilee Singers, the other minor songs either having no sixth or having the leading-tone. A fine example in my manuscript collection excited the admiration of M. Tiersot, who sets it down in his brochure as an illustration of the first Gregorian tone. It is a revival hymn, "Come tremble-ing down," and in it the "wood-

[1] See "Come tremble-ing down," page 85.
[2] See page 86.

"Come trembleing down"

Allegretto

Come tremble-ing down, go shout-ing home, Safe in the sweet arms of

Je - sus, Come Je - sus; 'Twas just a-bout the break of day, King Je-sus stole my

heart a-way; 'Twas just a-bout the break of day, King Je-sus stole my heart a-way.

una corda

A spiritual from Boyle Co., Kentucky, transcribed from the singing of a former slave for the author by Miss Mildred J. Hill, of Louisville. A fine example of the raised sixth in the minor mode. Arranged by the author.

You May Bury Me in de Eas'

2. Father Gabriel in dat day,
He'll take wings and fly away,
For to hear de trumpet soun'
In dat mornin'.
You may bury him, etc.

3. Good ole Christians in dat day,
Dey'll take wings and fly away,
etc.

4. Good ole preachers in dat day,
Dey'll take wings, etc.

5. In dat dreadful judgmen' day
I'll take wings, etc.

Melody from "The Story of the Jubilee Singers"; arrangement for this work by H.T. Burleigh. One of the finest examples extant of the effect of the major sixth in the minor mode.

[86]

note wild" has a barbaric shout of jubilation to which
correct verbal accent has been sacrificed:

> Come tremble-ing down, go shouting home,
> Safe in the sweet arms of Jesus.
> 'Twas just about the break *of* day
> King Jesus stole my heart away.

Concerning the text of this song it may be said that it
is scarcely to be wondered at that the amorous sentiment
of many Methodist and Baptist revival hymns finds its
echo in the hymns of the negroes.

The interval containing three semitones, which the in-
ventors of modern Occidental harmony avoided by arbi-
trary alteration of the minor scale, is so marked an element
in the music of Southeastern Europe and Western Asia
that the scale on which much of this music is based is
called the Oriental scale in the books. It is found in the
melodies of the Arabs, of the peoples of the Balkan peninsula, of the Poles and Magyars. The ancient synagogal
hymns of the Jews are full of it. In some cases it results
from raising the fourth interval of the minor scale; in
others from raising the seventh. In many cases, of which
the "Rakoczy March" is a familiar and striking example,
the interval occurs twice. The peculiar wailing effect of
the Oriental scale, most noticeable when the intervals are
sounded in descending order, is also to be heard in the song
of the priestesses and their dance in "Aida" and in Rubinstein's song, "Der Asra."

One of the songs in my manuscript collection shows a
feeling for the augmented, or superfluous second, as
Engel calls it, though the interval is not presented directly
to the eye or ear because of the absence of a tone which is
a constituent part of it—the sixth. It is the baptismal
hymn, "Freely Go" (see page 88), which makes a startling
effect with its unprepared beginning on the leading-tone.
An instance of the creation of the interval by the raising
of the fourth is found in the extremely interesting song
"Father Abraham," in the arrangement of which Mr.
Burleigh has retained the effect of a unique choral accompaniment as sung at the Calhoun school. (See page 90.)
Notable, too, in this song is the appreciation of tone-

Baptizing Hymn

Ev -'ry time I look up to the House of God, The

An - gels cry out Glo - ry! Glo-ry be to my God who

lives on high! To save a soul from dan ger.

From Boyle Co., Kentucky. Collected for the author by Miss Mildred J. Hill, of Louisville; harmonized by Henry Holden Huss. An extraordinary instance of a feeling for the scale of Oriental peoples, with its augmented second. The effect of this interval may be observed by sounding D-sharp, C and B at the beginning. The interval of the sixth, C, is sedulously avoided in the minor portion of the melody.

Father Abraham
"Tell it"

Father Abraham sittin' down side-a ob de ho-ly Lamb, 'Way up on de moun-tain-top; My Lord spoke an' de char-iot stop, Sit-tin' down side-a ob de ho-ly Lamb; Fa-ther A-bra-ham sit-tin' down side-a ob de ho-ly Lamb.

Tell it, tell it, tell it, tell it tell it, tell it, tell it, tell it!

Words and melody from "Calhoun Plantation Songs". Collected and edited by Emily Hallowell (Boston, C. W. Thompson & Co.). Published here by permission. Arranged by H. T. Burleigh. An example of the use of the Oriental interval called the augmented, or superfluous second (C♯ - B♭).

painting exemplified in the depiction of the sojourn on the mountain-top by persistent reiteration of the highest note reached by the melody.

I have no disposition to indulge in speculations touching the origin of either the conventional scales or the departures from them which I have pointed out in these songs. There are other variations, but they do not present themselves in sufficient numbers or in a sufficiently marked manner to justify their discussion as characteristic of the music of the people who employed them. They may be sporadic and due only to some personal equation in the singer who sang them to the collector. In no case, however, do they occur in songs which are commonplace in structure or sentiment. I should like to say that the melodies which seem to be based on the Oriental scale prove the persistence in the Afro-American folksongs of an element, or idiom, retained from their original Eastern home or derived from intercourse between the ancestors of the black slaves and some of the peoples of western Asia to whom the scale is native; but to make such an assertion would be unscientific; we lack the support here of such a body of evidence as we have to prove the African origin of the aberrations from the major scale which I have discussed. Nevertheless, it is significant in my eyes that the few songs which were gathered for me by Miss Hill in Kentucky and the songs collected by Miss Hallowell also presented themselves to the apprehension, though not to the comprehension, of the collectors of the "Slave Songs of the United States." The intermediate collectors—those who made the Fisk and Hampton collections—having a more popular purpose in view were, I fear, indifferent to their value and beauty.

It is a pity that students are without adequate material from which the natural history of the scales might be deduced—a pity and a wrong. Governments and scientific societies backed by beneficent wealth are spending enormous sums in making shows out of our museums. For these shows men go to Africa actuated by the savage propensity to kill, and call its gratification scientific research. Who has gone to Africa to capture a melody? No one. Yet a few scores or hundreds of phonographic records of music would be worth more to science and art to-day than a thousand stuffed skins of animals robbed of life by the bullets of a Roosevelt.

It is unfortunate that musical scholars are unable, for want of material, to deduce a sound theory concerning the origin of the scale; it is also unfortunate that a knowledge of African languages and dialects does not come to our assistance in accounting for the most marked rhythmical characteristic of the songs of the American negroes. This characteristic is found in the use of a figure in which the emphasis is shifted from the strong to the weak part of a time-unit by making the first note of two into which the beat is divided take only a fraction of the time of the second. This effect of propulsion when frequently repeated becomes very stirring, not to say exciting, and, as has been disclosed by the development of "ragtime," leads to a sort of rhythmical intoxication exemplified in the use of the device not only in the first beat of a measure, but in the other beats also, and even in the fractional divisions of a beat, no matter how small they have been made. When this species of syncopation, known as the Scotch, or Scot's, snap, or catch, became popular in the Italian opera airs of the eighteenth century it was held to be the offspring of a device commonly found in the popular music of Scotland. It is a characteristic element of the Strathspey reel, and the belief has been expressed that it got into vocal music from the fact that Burns and other poets wrote words for Scottish dance-tunes. "It was in great favor with many of the Italian composers of the eighteenth century," says J. Muir Wood (writing in Grove's "Dictionary of Music and Musicians") "for Burney, who seems to have invented the name, says in his account of the Italian opera in London, in 1748, that 'there was at this time too much of the Scotch catch, or cutting short of the first two notes in a melody.' He blames Cocchi, Perez and Jommelli, all three masters concerned in the opera 'Vologeso,' for being lavish of the snap." Adding to his article on the subject in the second edition of Grove's work, he says: "In the hands of Hook and other purveyors of the psuedo-Scottish music which was in vogue at Vauxhall and elsewhere in the eighteenth century, it became a senseless vulgarism, and, with the exception of a few songs . . . and the Strathspey reel, in which it is an essential feature, its presence may generally be accepted as proof that the music in which it occurs is not genuine."

What Wood here remarks about the pseudo-Scotch music of the eighteenth century as it was cultivated in the music halls may be said of latter-day "ragtime," which, especially in the "turkey-trot" and "tango" dances, monopolizes the music almost to the exclusion of melody and harmony. There is no reason why drums and gongs should not give these dances all the musical impulse they need. Though it is at the expense of a digression, it is not out of place to point out that in this year of pretended refinement, which is the year of our Lord 1913, the dance which is threatening to force grace, decorum and decency out of the ballrooms of America and England is a survival of African savagery, which was already banished from the plantations in the days of slavery. It was in the dance that the bestiality of the African blacks found its frankest expression. The Cuban Habanera, which has an African rhythmical foundation (the melodic superstructure having been reared by the white natives of the southern countries of America), grew into the most graceful and most polite of the Creole dances. Concerning it and its depraved ancestor, the tango, Friedenthal says in his "Musik, Tanz und Dichtung bei den Kreolen Amerikas":

But the habanera is not only danced by the cultivated creoles, but also by preference in the West Indies by the colored plebs. In such cases not a trace of grace is longer to be found; on the contrary, the movements of the dances leave nothing to be desired in the line of unequivocal obscenity. It is this vulgar dance, popularly called tango (after an African word "tangana"), which sought vainly to gain admission to our salons under the title of "tango argentino," by way of Argentina. It was shown to the lower classes of Argentina last year—the jubilee year of the republic. To the honor of the great country on the Silver River it may be said at once that there the habanera is never danced except in the most decent form. It is indubitable, however, that the Cuban tango was the original product and the danza-habanera its refined copy prepared for cultured circles, the creoles having borrowed not only the rhythms but also the choregraphic movements of the dances from the Africans.

It can scarcely be set down to the credit of American and English women that in adopting the tango they are imitating the example, not of the ladies of Argentina, but of the women of the Black Republic. Friedenthal says:

The Haytian salon dance, Méringue, is identical with the danza of the Spanish islands; but there is this difference, that even in the higher circles of Port-au-Prince, in which decorum and tact prevail and where the young, light colored women are of fascinating amiability, the gestures of the dance are never so unobjectionable as is the case with the Spanish creoles; from which it is to be seen that the dance, consciously or unconsciously, has a different purpose among these peoples. All the more undisguised is the crude sensuality among the lower classes of the Haytian population. Here every motion is obscene; and I am not at all considering the popular merrymakings or dance festivals secretly held partly in the open, partly in the forests, which are more like orgies, in which the African savagery, which has outlived centuries, has unbridled expression.

The rhythmical device under discussion is also found in the popular music of Hungary, where it is called *alla zoppa* (limping). Here it is unquestionably the product of poetry. Dr. Aurel Wachtel, discussing the music of the Magyars[1]—says that the rhythmical construction of their ballads is most closely allied to the peculiarity of the Magyar language, which distinguishes the short and long syllables much more sharply than any other language spoken by the peoples of Germanic-Slavic-Romanic origin. The character of the Magyar tongue does not tolerate that prosodically long syllables in song shall be used as short, or *vice versa*.

Now, whether the rhythms of dance-music be derived from the songs which gave time to the feet of the original dancers, or the rhythms of poetry were borrowed from the steps of the dance, it would seem as if the determining factor was the word. The most primitive music was vocal. Poetical song had its origin in improvization, and improvization would be clogged unless musical and verbal rhythm could flow together. The rhythmical snap of the American negroes is in all likelihood an aboriginal relic, an idiom which had taken so powerful a hold on them that they carried it over into their new environment, just as they did the melodic peculiarities which I have investigated. It was so powerful an impulse, indeed, that it broke down

[1] "Musikalisches Wochenblatt," July 5, 1878.

the barriers interposed by the new language which they were compelled to adopt in their new home. For the sake of the snap the creators of the folksongs of the American negroes did not hesitate to distort the metrical structure of their lines. In scores upon scores of instances trochees like "Moses," "Satan," "mother," "brother," "sister," and so forth, become iambs, while dactyls become amphibrachys, like "No*body*," "No*body* knows" (see page 96), "These *are* my," "No *one* can," etc. A glance into any one of the collections mentioned will furnish examples by the score. Of the 527 songs examined, 315 contain the rhythmical snap which is as well entitled to be called African as Scottish.

"Another noticeable feature of the songs," says Theodore F. Seward in his preface to the Fisk Jubilee collection, "is the rare occurence of triple time, or three-part measure, among them. The reason for this is doubtless to be found in the beating of the foot and the swaying of the body, which are such frequent accompaniments of the singing. These motions are in even measure and in perfect time; and so it will be found that however broken and seemingly irregular the movement of the music, it is always capable of the most exact measurement."

Triple time is, indeed, of extremely rare occurence in the melodies; taking as a standard the collection to which my observations have been directed, less than one-tenth of the tunes are in simple and compound triple time. The regular swaying of the body to which Mr. Seward refers might better be described as an effect than as a cause of the even movement of the music. It is no doubt an inherited predilection, a survival of a primitive march-rhythm which, in the nature of the case, lies at the bottom of the first communal movements of primitive peoples; uneven measure is more naturally associated with a revolving movement, of which I find no mention in the notes of my African reading. The "shout" of the slaves, as we have seen, was a march—circular only because that is the only kind of march which will not carry the dancers away from the gathering-place. Pantomimic dances, like those which I

Nobody Knows the Trouble I See

Nobody knows the trouble I see, Lord, Nobody knows the trouble I see; Nobody knows the trouble I see, Lord, Nobody knows but Je-sus. Brothers, will you pray for me, Brothers, will you pray for me, Brothers, will you pray for me, And help me to drive old Satan a-way?

* On repetition, "Sisters", "Mothers", "Preachers".
Words and melody from "The Story of the Jubilee Singers with their Songs", by J. B. T. Marsh.
Arrangement by the Author.

witnessed in the Dahoman village at the Columbian Exhibition, in 1893, are generally martial and consist of advances and retreats in linear formation with descriptive gestures.

The innate rhythmical capacity of the Africans has been sufficiently dwelt upon. In the American songs it finds its expression in the skill with which the negroes constrain their poetry to accept the rhythms of the music. Two authors, the Rev. J. Richardson and the Rev. James Sibree, jr. (the former of whom wrote on the hymnology of the Malagasy, the latter on their children's games and songs), agree (assuming that Wallaschek has quoted them correctly) in the statement that the poetry of the natives of Madagascar is not rhythmical, though their music is. Mr. Allen writes, in his preface to the "Slave Songs": "The negroes keep exquisite time in singing, and do not suffer themselves to be daunted by any obstacle in the words. The most obstinate scripture phrases or snatches from hymns they will force to do duty with any tune they please, and will dash heroically through a trochaic tune at the head of a column of iambs with wonderful skill." A glance into any collection of Afro-American songs will provide examples of Mr. Allen's meaning; but if the reader wishes to see how an irregular line can be made to evolve a characteristically rhythmic musical phrase he need but look in "O'er the Crossing" (pages 98-99), at the line "Keep praying! I do believe." Despite its rudeness, this song, because of its vivid imagery, comes pretty near to being poetry of the genuine type. To learn what word it was that in the process of oral transmission became corrupted into "waggin' " I have hunted and pondered in vain. Perhaps "We're a long time waggin' at the crossin' " was originally "We're a long time lagging at the crossing." Perhaps the word was once "waggoning." In the song "My body rock 'long fever,"[1] is a line, "Better true be long time get over crosses," which may have reflected a similar idea, though it is all vague now. In "I've been toilin' at de hill so long" of the Hampton collection there seems to be another parallel; but the song is very inferior.

[1] "Slave Songs," No. 45.

[97]

O'er the Crossing

pray-in', I do believe We're a long time waggin' o' de cross-in'. Keep

pray-in', I do believe We'll git home to heaven bime - by.

2. O yonder's my old mudder,
   Been a-waggin' at the hill so long;
   It's about time she cross over,
   Git home bime-by.
   Keep prayin', I do believe, etc.

3. O hear dat lumberin' thunder
   A-roll from do' to do',
   A callin' de people home to God;
   Dey'll git home bime-by.
   Little chil'n, I do believe, etc.

4. O see dat forked lightnin'
   A-jump from cloud to cloud,
   A-pickin' up God's chil'n;
   Dey'll git home bime-by.
   Pray, mourner, I do believe, etc.

Words and melody from "Slave Songs of the United States"; arranged for the author by Arthur Mees. The following note on the song appears in the collection from which it was taken: "This 'infinitely quaint description of the length of the heavenly road', as Col. Higginson styles it, is one of the most peculiar and wide-spread of the spirituals. It was sung as given above in Caroline Co., Virginia, and probably spread southward from this state variously modified in different localities."

CHAPTER VIII

STRUCTURAL FEATURES OF THE POEMS—FUNERAL MUSIC

IMPROVIZATION—SOLO AND CHORAL REFRAIN—EXAMPLES
FROM AFRICA—STRANGE FUNERAL CUSTOMS—THEIR
SAVAGE PROTOTYPES—MESSAGES TO THE DEAD—
GRAVEYARD SONGS OF THE AMERICAN
SLAVES

The general structure of the simpler (and therefore older) American songs shows a stanza containing an alternating solo verse and refrain, with sometimes a chorus. "The most common arrangement," say the editors of "Slave Songs," in their directions for singing, "gives the second and fourth lines to the refrain and the first and third to the verse; and in this case the third line may be a repetition of the first or may have different words. Often, however, the refrain occupies only one line, the verse occupying the other three, while in one or two songs the verse is only one line, while the refrain is three lines in length. The refrain is repeated with each stanza; the words of the verse are changed at the pleasure of the leader, or fugleman, who sings either well-known words, or, if he is gifted that way, invents verses as the song goes on. In addition to the stanza, some of the songs have a chorus, which usually consists of a fixed set of words, though in some of the songs the chorus is a good deal varied. The refrain of the main stanza often appears in the chorus."

There is nothing peculiar to these American folksongs in this recurrent refrain, but it is worth noticing that the feature in the form of an alternating line of improvization and a reiterated burden is found throughout Africa. "Their style is the recitative broken by a full chorus," says Sir Richard Burton, speaking of the people of the lake region of Central Africa. Carl Mauch, in his "Reisen in Süd-Afrika" says of the music of the Makalaka that it usually consists of a phrase of eight measures, repeated *ad infinitum*, to which are sung improvized verses with a refrain. Wallaschek cites Eduard Mohr[1] as saying that the Damaras rarely dance, in fact, only on extraordinary occasions; and they sing together just as rarely, although fond of solo singing, the words for which they extemporize, while the refrains are taken up by a chorus. Wallaschek also says (page 4), "The Balatpi reminded Weber[2] of Venetian gondoliers or of the lazzaroni in Naples. One would improvise a stanza which others would immediately sing in chorus to a charming melody. Each in turn improvises thus, so that all have an opportunity of exhibiting their talents for poetry and wit. The fact that all words ended in a vowel sound simplified the extemporization of verses, which are not invariably accurate as regards rhythm. The general singing of these stanzas seemed to afford the greatest amusement to the singers as they sat in a circle around the campfire." In "Across Africa," by Verney Lovett Cameron, C. B., D. C. L.,[3] we read this of the fortune-telling by a fetich man: "On arrival he seated himself on the ground, surrounded by his friends, and then commenced a monotonous recitative. In this he accompanied himself by shaking a rattle made of basketwork shaped like a dumbbell, while the circle of attendants joined in a chorus, sometimes striking their bells and at others laying them down and clapping their hands in a kind of rhythmic cadence."

Speaking of the Zulu-Kafirs, the Rev. Louis Grout says in Chapter XIV of his book "Zulu-Land; or, Life Among the Zulu-Kafirs of Natal and Zulu-Land":[4]

The most of their songs consist of only a few words, which they repeat over and over again with such variations as their national taste and habit or individual fancy may dictate. . . . Their songs often have a special fitness for the occasion, as when a man in search of a cow goes humming:

[1] "Nach den Victoriafällen des Zambesi," I, 160.
[2] Ernst von Weber, "Vier Jahre in Afrika," I, 221.
[3] New York, Harpers, 1877.
[4] Philadelphia: The Presbyterian Publication Company, 1864.

"Ma i ze inkomo yetu, si ya yi biza;
Si ti, ma i ze, ma i zeka;
Ma i ze kumi, ma i zeke;
Ma i ze inkomo yetu, si ya yi biza."

That is:

"Our cow, let her come, we are calling her;
We say, let her come, let her come, so let her come;
Let her come to me, then let her come;
Our cow, let her come, we are calling her."

Several natives spent a rainy day hard at work digging out and killing three or four porcupines which had made them trouble in their gardens; and the next morning one of them passed my door singing the following song, which I was told he indited for the occasion:

"Truly, oh, truly, they'll perish anon.
The land of the Zulu so slyly they leave.
All the people, they come, they come,
The land of the Zulu so slyly they leave.
Truly, oh, truly," etc.

From Denham and Clapperton's "Narrative of Travels in Northern and Central Africa,"[1] Carl Engel quotes the following extemporaneous song of negro bards in Bornou in praise of their Sultan:

Give flesh to the hyenas at daybreak—
Oh, the broad spears!
The spear of the Sultan is the broadest—
Oh, the broad spears!
I behold thee now—I desire to see none other—
Oh, the broad spears!
My horse is as tall as a high wall—
Oh, the broad spears!
He will fight against ten—he fears nothing!
Oh, the broad spears!
He has slain ten; the guns are yet behind—
Oh, the broad spears!
The elephant of the forest brings me what I want—
Oh, the broad spears!
Like unto thee, so is the Sultan—
Oh, the broad spears!
Be brave! Be brave, my friends and kinsmen—
Oh, the broad spears!
God is great! I wax fierce as a beast of prey—
Oh, the broad spears!
God is great! To-day those I wished for are come—
Oh, the broad spears!

It would be an easy matter to multiply parallels of this song in the matter of form from among the religious songs of the American negroes. Let two suffice:

I want to be my fader's chil'en—
Roll, Jordan, roll!
O say, ain't you done wid de trouble ob de world?
Roll, Jordan, roll!

[1] London, 1826, II, 19.

[102]

I ask de Lord how long I hold 'em—
    Roll, Jordan, roll!
My sins so heavy I can't get along. Ah!
    Roll, Jordan, roll!
I cast my sins in de middle ob de sea—
    Roll, Jordan, roll!

Here the second:

Hurry on, my weary soul—
    And I yearde from heaven to-day!
My sin is forgiven and my soul set free—
    And I yearde from heaven to-day!
A baby born in Bethlehem—
    And I yearde from heaven to-day!
De trumpet sound in de odder bright land—
    And I yearde from heaven to-day!
My name is called and I must go—
    And I yearde from heaven to-day!
De bell is a-ringin' in de odder bright world—
    And I yearde from heaven to-day!

Relics of ancient ceremonies connected with death and burial have survived amongst the American negroes and have been influential in producing some strangely beautiful and impressive songs. One of these, "Dig My Grave" (see page 104), from the Bahamas, where the songs, though they have much community of both poetical and musical phrase with them, yet show a higher development than do the slave songs of the States, is peculiarly impressive. The first period of its melody—it might be called tripartite —is fairly Schumannesque in breadth and dignity. Another, "I Look o'er Yander (see page 105), is not comparable with it from a musical point of view, but derives peculiar interest from the ceremony with which it is associated. This function is one of those which I call a relic of ancient ceremonies, because, like the peculiar idioms of the melodies, it cannot have been copied from any of the funeral rites which the slaves saw among their white masters, but does show affinity with Old World and oldtime ceremonies.

Like the ancient Romans, the slaves were in the habit of burying their dead at night. Like their savage ancestors in Africa, they expressed their sorrow in nocturnal song. It is remotely possible, too, that once they indulged in funeral dances, even in such wild orgies as travellers have described. These dances, like most others, have passed

Dig My Grave

Words and melody from "Bahama Songs and Stories," by Charles. L. Edwards, Ph. D., published for the American Folk-Lore Society by Houghton, Mifflin & Co., Boston, and reprinted by permission. The arrangement made for this book by H. T. Burleigh.

I Look o'er Yander
(Bahama)

An "anthem" which is sung in the Bahamas at a "settin' up"- a sort of all-night watch in and around the hut of a dying person. Words and melody from "Bahama Songs and Stories", by Charles L. Edwards, Ph. D., published for the American Folk-Lore Society by Houghton,Mifflin & Co. and reprinted by permission. The arrangement made for this work by H. T. Burleigh.

[105]

away in communities in which Protestant influences were dominant, especially where the teachings of the Methodists and Baptists took strongest hold. There the "shout" provided vent for the emotions to which their ancestors gave expression in mad and lascivious dancing.

Paul B. du Chaillu[1] describes a nocturnal funeral chant whose wailing seemed burdened with a sense of absolute hopelessness and whose words ran thus:

> Oh, you will never speak to us any more,
> We can not see your face any more,
> You will never walk with us again,
> You will never settle our palavers for us.

Edwards, in his history of the West Indies,[2] says of the slaves in those islands:

> At other times, more especially at the burial of such among them as were respected in life or venerable through age, they exhibit a sort of Pyrrhick or war-like dance, in which their bodies are strongly agitated by running, leaping and jumping, with many violent and frantick gestures and contortions. Their funeral songs, too, are all of the heroick or martial cast, affording some colour to the prevalent notion that the negroes consider death not only as a welcome and happy release from the calamities of their condition, but also as a passport to the place of their nativity; a deliverance which, while it frees them from bondage, returns them to the society of their dearest, long lost and lamented relatives in Africa.

From the description by Francisco Travassos Valdez,[3] it appears that in Loanda, Lower Guinea, when a death occurs the friends of the dead person not only sing and dance at the funeral, but repeat the rites at intervals of a week and a month. In the songs the good deeds of the departed are celebrated and his virtues extolled. The eulogies are interrupted at intervals by one of the mourners exclaiming, "He is dead!" whereupon all the others reply in chorus, "Woe is me!"

In some sections of Africa the period of mourning is, or was, a period of cessation from musical performances; in

[1] The song is quoted by Prof. Edwards from Du Chaillu's "Explorations and Adventures in Equatorial Africa," and Prof. Edwards refers for similar examples to Major A. G. Laing's "Travels in Western Africa," London, 1825, pp. 233 and 237; Theodor Waitz's "Anthropologie der Naturvölker," Leipsic, 1860, II, pp. 240 and 243; and K. Endemann's "Mittheilungen über die Sotho-Neger," Berlin, 1874, pp. 57, 63.

[2] "The History, Civil and Commercial, of the British Colonies in the West Indies," by Bryan Edwards, Esq., F. R. S., S. A., Vol. II, p. 103.

[3] "Six Years of a Traveller's Life in Western Africa," London, 1861, cited by Engel.

others death and burial were accompanied by noisy lamentations.

The Abbé Proyart, in his "History of Loango, Kakongo and Other Kingdoms of Africa,"[1] tells of a custom, when a native is sick, of summoning, with the physician, a band of musicians, who assemble around his house and play on instruments incessantly day and night, presumably till the patient is recovered or dead. It is not unlikely that in this custom (which, in a way, suggests the practices of the shamans of the North American Indians) is to be found the origin of the singular custom of "settin' up," which is described by Professor Charles L. Edwards in his "Bahama Songs and Stories." This nocturnal song-service, which Jenny Woodville described as a feature of slave life in the Southern States,[2] is held when a negro is supposed to be dying. "The singers, men, women and children of all ages," says Professor Edwards, "sit about on the floor of the larger room of the hut and stand outside at the doors and windows, while the invalid lies upon the floor in the smaller room. Long into the night they sing their most mournful hymns and 'anthems,' and only in the light of dawn do those who are left as chief mourners silently disperse."

The "anthem" which is most often used on these occasions is "I Look o'er Yander." A notable thing about it is that it is one of the rare examples of a negro melody in three-part measure (compound); but there is no suggestion of a lightsome mood on that account in the melody. "With all the sad intonation accented by the tense emotion of the singers," says Professor Edwards, "it sounds in the distance as though it might well be the death triumph of some old African chief:

Each one of the dusky group, as if by intuition, takes some part in the melody, and the blending of all tone-colors in the soprano, tenor, alto and bass, without reference to the fixed laws of harmony, makes such peculiarly touching music as I have never heard elsewhere. As this song of consolation accompanies the sighs of the dying one, it seems to be taken up by the mournful rustle of the palm and to be lost only in the undertone of murmur from the distant coral reef. It is all weird and intensely sad.

[1] In the Pinkert Collection.
[2] "Lippincott's Magazine" for November, 1878.

Closely related to this custom of "settin' up" apparently is one to which Mrs. Jeannette Robinson Murphy called attention in an interesting article, accompanied by songs and stories, which she published some years ago in "The Independent." In this custom the hymns which are sung at the deathbed become messages to loved ones gone before, which the departing soul is charged to bear to heaven. "When a woman dies," wrote Mrs. Murphy, "some friend or relative will kneel down and sing to the soul as it takes its flight. One of the songs contains endless verses, conveying remembrances to relatives in glory." Here, surely, is a lovely and truly exalted variant of the primitive custom of placing coins in the mouths of the dead to pay the Stygian ferryman, or slaughtering dogs, horses and slaves for a chief's companionship on the journey into the next world.

And yet even this affecting ceremony may have had its origin in the awful practice which prevails in Dahomey, to which every year a large number of lives are, or used to be, sacrificed. On the death of a Dahoman king the "grand custom," as it is called, is celebrated, at which at times as many as five hundred captives have been slain to make up the household of the departed monarch in the other world. Besides this sacrifice there is an annual one at which from sixty to eighty are killed and sent as bearers of messages and news from the new king to his predecessor. Into the ear of each unfortunate the king whispers the words which he wishes to have reported, whereupon the executioner immediately strikes off the ghostly postman's mortal head.

Much more singular than this singing to the soul, is a custom which is said to have prevailed in South Carolina, where, on the death of the father of a family, his relatives, assembled around the coffin, ranged in order of age and relationship, sang the following hymn while marching around the body:

Dese all my fader's children.
Outshine de sun!
My fader's done wid de trouble o' de world—
Outshine de sun!

The youngest child was then taken and passed first over, then under the coffin, whereupon two men took it on their shoulders and carried it to the grave *"on the run."*[1]

Among the songs which Colonel Higginson imprisoned in his notebook—writing it down, perhaps, in the darkness, with his hand, as he says, in the covert of his pocket, as he overheard it from dusky figures moving in "the rhythmical barbaric chant called a 'shout' " beside the campfire, then carrying it to his tent "like a captured bird or insect" —was a nocturnal funeral song which surprised him most because its images were furnished directly by external nature. "With all my experience of their ideal ways of speech," he says, "I was startled when first I came on such a flower of poetry in the dark soil."

> I know moonlight, I know starlight;
>   I lay dis body down.
> I walk in de moonlight, I walk in de starlight;
>   I lay dis body down.
> I know de graveyard, I know de graveyard,
>   When I lay dis body down.
> I walk in de graveyard, I walk troo de graveyard
>   To lay dis body down.
> I lay in de grave and stretch out my arms;
>   I lay dis body down.
> I go to de judgment in de evenin' of de day
>   When I lay dis body down.
> An' my soul an' your soul will meet in de day
>   When we lay dis body down.

And Colonel Higginson comments: " 'I'll lie in de grave and stretch out my arms.' Never, it seems to me, since man first lived and suffered, was his infinite longing for peace uttered more plaintively than in that line." The phrase of melody which the editors of "Slave Songs" appended to Colonel Higginson's words is altogether too banal to be accepted as the one to which a poem bearing such a burden of pathos could possibly have been sung. The music is much more likely to have been something like that of "O Graveyard" (see page 110), which I have included in my list—the words a variant of "O Moonrise," the tune quite worthy of being described as a flower of melody floating on dark waters in the shifting shadows of the moon:

[1] "Slave Songs," page 101.

O Graveyard!

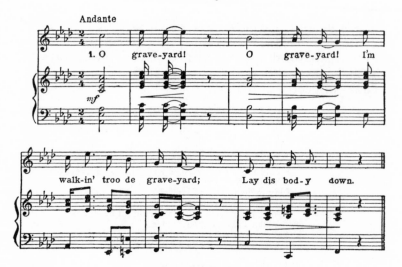

1. O grave-yard! O grave-yard! I'm walk-in' troo de grave-yard; Lay dis bod-y down.

2. I know moonlight, I know starlight,
   I'm walkin' troo de starlight;
   Lay dis body down.

3. O my soul! O your soul!
   I'm walkin' troo de graveyard;
   Lay dis body down.

The arrangement made for this work by H. T. Burleigh. Words and melody from "Slave Songs of the United States," New York, 1867.

> O graveyard! O graveyard!
> I'm walkin' troo de graveyard—
> Lay dis body down.

It was Mr. Allen's ingenious surmise that this was the song which was heard by Mr. W. H. Russell, war correspondent of the London "Times" and which he described in Chapter XVIII of "My Diary, North and South." He is telling of a midnight row from Potaligo to "Mr. Trewcott's Estate" on Barnwell Island:

The oarsmen, as they bent to their task, beguiled the way by singing in unison a real negro melody, which was as unlike the works of the Ethiopian Serenaders as anything in song could be unlike another. It was a barbaric sort of madrigal, in which one singer beginning was followed by the others in unison, repeating the refrain in chorus, and full of quaint expression and melancholy:

> Oh, your soul! Oh, my soul!
> I'm going to the churchyard
> To lay this body down;
>
> Oh, my soul! Oh, your soul!
> We're going to the churchyard
> To lay this nigger down.

And then some appeal to the difficulty of passing the "Jawdan" constituted the whole of the song, which continued with unabated energy during the whole of the little voyage. To me it was a strange scene. The stream, dark as Lethe, flowing between the silent, houseless, rugged banks, lighted up near the landing by the fire in the woods, which reddened the sky—the wild strain and the unearthly adjurations to the singer's souls as though they were palpable, put me in mind of the fancied voyage across the Styx.

CHAPTER IX

DANCES OF THE AMERICAN NEGROES

CREOLE MUSIC—THE EFFECT OF SPANISH INFLUENCES—
OBSCENITY OF NATIVE AFRICAN DANCES—RELICS IN
THE ANTILLES—THE HABANERA—DANCE-TUNES
FROM MARTINIQUE

The world over there is a most intimate relationship between folksong and folkdance. Poetical forms and rhythms are the effects as well as the causes of the re-gulated movements and posings of the dance. Peoples, like those of Africa, who have a highly developed sense of rhythm also have a passionate fondness for the dance, and it was to have been expected that the black slaves would not only develop them in their new environment, but also preserve the rhythms of those primitive dances in the folksongs which they created here. This was the case, in a measure, but the influence which was most potent in the development of the characteristic folksong was prejudicial to the dance.

The dances which were part and parcel of the primitive superstitions which the slaves brought with them from Africa necessarily fell under the ban of the Christian Church, especially of its Protestant branch. In Louisiana, the Antilles and Spanish America the Roman Catholic Church exercised a restrictive and reformative influence upon the dance; in other parts of the continent the Metho-dist and Baptist denominations, whose systems were most appealing to the emotional nature of the blacks, rooted it out altogether, or compelled the primitive impulse to find expression in the "shout"—just as the same influences led the white population to substitute the song-games, which are now confined to children, for the dance in many sections of the United States.

[112]

DANCES OF THE AMERICAN NEGROES

Practically all of the dances described by African travellers were orgies in which the dramatic motif, when not martial, was lascivious. Dr. Holub, in his "Seven Years in South Africa,"[1] says that the Mabunda dance is of so objectionable a character that the negroes refuse to dance it, except in masks. In "From Benguela to the Territory of Yucca," by H. Capello and R. Ivens, of the Royal Portuguese Navy,[2] the authors say of the native dances: "As a rule, these are of the grossest kind, which the women, more particularly, try to make as obscene as possible; without grace, without cachet, but simply indecent and fitted only to inflame the passions of the lowest of our sex. After three or four pirouttes before the spectators, the male dancer butts his stomach violently against the nearest female, who, in turn, repeats the action, and thus brings the degrading spectacle to an end." Dr. Georg Schweinfurth, in his "Heart of Africa,"[3] describing an orgy of the Bongo, says: "The license of their revelry is of so gross a character that the representations of one of my interpreters must needs be suppressed. It made a common market-woman droop her eyes, and called up a blush even to the poor sapper's cheeks." In "Across Africa," by Verney Lovett Cameron, C. B., D. C. L., commander in the Royal Navy,[4] the author writes: "Dancing in Manyuema"—a cannibal country—"is a prerogative of the chiefs. When they feel inclined for a terpsichorean performance they single out a good-looking woman from the crowd, and the two go through much wriggling and curious gesticulation opposite each other. The village drums are brought out and vigorously beaten, the drummers meanwhile shouting 'Gamello! Gamello!' If the woman is unmarried the fact of a chief asking her to dance is equivalent to an offer of marriage, and many complications often occur in consequence."

There was none of this bestiality on exhibition in the dances of the Dahomans, which I saw at the World's

[1] London, 1881.
[2] London, 1882.
[3] Vol. I, page 355.
[4] New York: Harper's, 1887.

[113]

Fair in Chicago in 1893, for reasons which can easily be imagined; such spectacles as the travellers describe would not be tolerated in a civilized community anywhere in the world at the present time, though the equally frank *danse du ventre*, which the Latin satirists scourged centuries ago, was to be seen in the Midway Plaisance under circumstances which seemed to have been accepted as a palliative, just as the "tango" and the "turkey-trot," the former African in name and both African in dramatic motif and purpose, are tolerated in circles which call themselves polite to-day. The dances of the Dahomans were war dances. These people have been in constant contact with white traders for more than a hundred years, but they probably take the same "delight in singing, dancing and cutting off heads" now that they did when Forbes visited them three-quarters of a century ago. Indeed, a bit of pantomimic action, which I saw repeated several times at the fair, testified, in a way almost too vivid to be amusing, to the love of decapitation which has been so much commented on by travellers.

A dozen or more names of dances, all of vague meaning and etymology, have come down to us in the books of men who have written about the negroes in the Western Hemisphere, and so far as can be learned all these dances were more or less wild and lascivious. Lascivious they have remained, even in the forms which they have assumed under the influence of French and Spanish culture. There is no doubt in the mind of Friedenthal, whose observations were wide and whose descriptions are sympathetic, that the rhythmical foundation of the fascinating Habanera is a negro product upon which graceful melodies were imposed. "We shall make no error," he writes,[1] in assuming that the Habanera, as its name already indicates, originated in Havana. Thence it conquered all of Spanish and Portugese America (*i. e.*, Brazil), and also the European settlements in the West Indies, Central and South America. But it is to be particularly observed that only the real Habanera, the dance with simple rhythms, penetrated

[1] Op. cit., pp. 115-116.

to these lands. Extended and complicated rhythms are known only where the negroes are to be found outside of the West Indies, in Brazil and on the coasts of Venezuela, Colombia, Central America and Mexico. In other countries, as, for instance, the interior of Mexico, the Plata states and Chili, where there are no negroes, extended and complicated rhythms are entirely unknown."

Commenting in another place[1] on the influences which created the dances of the American creoles, he says:

Not much less can have been the share, on the other hand, which the Spaniards and creoles took in the dances of the blacks. Every day in their hours of rest they had opportunities to see the partly sensual, partly grotesque and wild dances of their black slaves, and to hear their peculiar songs. What impressions may not these fascinating, complicated and bizarre and yet transparent rhythms of the negroes have made upon the Spaniards who themselves possess a refined sense of rhythm. Added to this the strange instruments of percussion which, while marking the rhythm, exerted an almost uncanny effect.

Here, then, two races confronted each other, both highly musical but reared in different musical worlds. No wonder that the Spaniards also benefited from and promptly took up these remarkable rhythms into their own music. Of all these rhythms, however, the simplest which can be heard from all negroes is this:

which, we have already learned, is the rhythm of the Habanera. The melody of the Habanera, which we would derive from Middle or Southern Spain, and the rhythm which accompanies it and had its origin in Africa, therefore represent, in a way, the union of Spanish spirit with African technique. We thus get acquainted with a hybrid art in the Habanera, or Danza, but as must at once be said here, the only hybrid art-form of creole music.

The Habanera, as a dance, is not vocal, but its form has been used most charmingly in vocal music, and in two of its manifestations, Carmen's air in the first scene of Bizet's opera and the Mexican song "Paloma,"

it is universally familiar. I have found a few Afro-American songs in which the characteristic rhythm is so persistently used as to suggest that they were influenced by a subconscious memory of the old dance; but the evidence

[1] Page 95.

is not sufficient to authorize such a statement as a scientific fact. I make room for one, "Tant sirop est doux," an erotic song from Martinique, which M. Tiersot says is widely known among French colonies inhabited by the blacks.

The origin of the Habanera is perpetuated in its name, and in this respect it stands alone. Other dances of which writers on the Antilles have made mention are the Bamboula, Bouèné, Counjai (or Counjaille), Calinda (or Calienda, possibly from the Spanish *Qué linda*), Bélé (from the French *bel air*), Benguine, Babouille, Cata (or Chata) and Guiouba. The last word seems preserved in the term "juba," which is now applied to the patting accompaniments of negro dance-songs made familiar by the old minstrel shows. The word Congo, as applied to a negro dance which is still remembered in Louisiana, is, I fancy, a generic term there, though it is also used in French Guiana for a dance called Chica in Santo Domingo and the Windward Islands. The Bamboula is supposed to have been so called after the drum of bamboo, which provided its musical stimulus. An African word seems to lie at the bottom of the term Counjai. Long years ago Lafcadio Hearn wrote me from New Orleans: "My quadroon neighbor, Mamzelle Eglantine, tells me that the word *Koundjo* (in the West Indies *Candio* or *Candjo*) refers to an old African dance which used to be danced with drums." Perhaps some such meaning is preserved in the Song "Criole Candjo." (See page 118.)

The etymology of the other terms baffles me, but it is of no consequence in this study; the dances were all alike in respect of the savage vigor and licentiousness which marked their performance. "The Calinda," say the editors of "Slave Songs of the United States," "was a sort of contradance which has now passed entirely out of use." Bescherelles describes the two lines as "*avançant et reculant en cadence et faisant des contortions fort singulières et des gestes fort lascifs.*" It is likely that the Calinda disappeared from Louisiana as a consequence of the prohibition of the dances in the Place Congo in New Orleans, about 1843;

Tant sirop est doux

Allegro risoluto

Tant sirop est doux, Made-lei-ne, Tant sirop est doux! doux! Ne

Ne

fai pas tant de bruit, Made-lein', ne fai pas tant de bruit, Madelein', La

cri-ez pas si fort, Made-lein', ne cri-ez pas si fort, Madelein',

mai-son n'est pas à nous, Made-lein', La mai-son n'est pas à nous.

A Martinique Song. Words and Melody collected by Lafcadio Hearn. Arrangement by the Author.

Criole Candjo

In- zou'   in zène Cri-
One day   one young Cre-

ole Cand - jo,   Belle pas - - sé blanc dan-
ole Can - dio,   Mo' fin - eh dan sho'

dan   là   yo,   Li té tout tans a - pé
nuff   white beau,   Kip all de time meck-in'

dire,_____   «Vi - ni, za - mie, pou' nous rire.»_____
free,_____   "Swit-hawt,meck mer - rie wid me."_____

2.

Mo courri dans youn bois voisin,
Mais Criole là prend même ci min,
Et tous tans li m'apé dire,
"Vini, zamie, pou' nous rire."
"Non, Miché, m'pas oulé rire moin,
Non, Miché, m'pas oulé rire."

3.

Mais li té tant cicané moi,
Pou li té quitté moin youn fois
Mo té 'blizé pou' li dire,
"Oui, Miché, mo oulé rire.
Oui, Miché, mo oulé rire moin,
Oui, Miché, mo oulé rire."

4.

Zaut tous qu'ap'ès rire moin là-bas
Si zaut te conne Candjo là,
Qui belle façon li pou' rire,
Djé pini moin! zaut s'ré dire,
"Oui, Miché, mo oulé rire moin,
Oui, Miché, mo oulé rire."

2.

(I go teck walk in wood close by,
But Creole teck same road and try
All time all time to meck free—
"Swithawt, meck merrie wid me."
"Naw, sah, I dawn't want meck merrie, me,
Naw, sah, I dawn't want meck merrie."

3.

But him slide 'round an 'round dis chile,
Tell, jis fo' sheck 'im off lill while
Me, I was bleedze fo' say: "Shoo!
If I'll meck merrie wid you?
O, yass, I ziss leave meck merrie, me,
Yass, sah, I ziss leave meck merrie."

4.

You-alls wat laugh at me so well,
I wish you'd knowed dat Creole swell,
Wid all 'is swit, smilin' trick.
'Pon my soul! you'd done say, quick,
"O, yass, I ziss leave meck merrie, me.
Yass, sah, I ziss leave meck merrie.")

The melody as written down by Mr. W. Macrum of Pittsburgh; English paraphrase by George W. Cable, used by his permission and that of The Century Company. A note to the author from Lafcadio Hearn (who, at that time, was a resident of New Orleans), says: "My quadroon neighbor, Mamzelle Eglantine, tells me that the word *koundjo* (in the West Indies *Candio* or *Candjo*) refers to an old African dance which used to be danced with drums. The 'Criole Candjo' is, therefore, a sort of nigger creole dandy who charms and cajoles women by his dancing—what the French would call *un beau valseur*."

but it and other dances of its character have remained in existence in the West Indies. Hearn says,[1] "Two old African dances, the *Caleinda* and the *Bélé* (which later is accompanied by chanted improvization) are danced on Sundays to the sound of the drum on almost every plantation in the island" (Martinique). As Hearn saw the Calinda it was danced by men only, all stripped to the waist and twirling heavy sticks in a mock fight. "Sometimes," he adds, "especially at the great village gatherings, when the blood becomes overheated by tafia, the mock fight may become a real one, and then even cutlasses are brought into play." The surmise lies near that the Calinda may originally have been a war dance. Its name and measures survive in some creole songs, one of which will occupy my attention when the use of song for satirical purposes is reached.

The Counjai ("Caroline," p. 139) evidently came under the personal observation of the lady who collected some secular creole songs in St. Charles Parish, La., which found their way into "Slave Songs of the United States." They were sung, she says, "to a simple sort of dance, a sort of minuet." But they are in duple time, while the minuet is in triple measure. The songs have a refrain, which is sung by the chorus, and solo verses which are improvized by a leader distinguished by his voice and poetical skill, who, in them, compliments a dusky beauty or lauds a plantation hero. The dancers do not sing, and the accompaniment seems to be purely instrumental—a mere beating on a drum made of a flour barrel and a rasping on the jawbone of an animal with a key. This singular instrument has a prototype in Africa in the shape of a notched board, which is rubbed with a stick. Livingstone describes what he calls a "cassuto," a "hollow piece of wood about a yard long, covered with a board cut like a ladder. Running a stick along it gives a sound within which passes for a tenor." The description is Wallaschek's; the Chinese have a temple instrument embodying the same principle—a wooden tiger with a serrated spine. Hearn mentions primitive drums as used

[1] "Two Years," etc., p. 143.

Aurore Pradère

trop zo - lie, Ya moun qui dit li pas po - lie; Tout
pret - ty, quite, Some folks they say she's not po - lite; All

D. C. al Fine

ça ya dit (Sia!) bin fou bin, C'est li mo ou - lé, c'est li ma pren.
this they say, no fool am I, For she's what I want, and her I'll have.

2. Aurore Pradère, belle 'ti fille, *(ter.)* Aurore Pradère, pretty maid, *(ter.)*
 C'est li mo oulé, c'est li ma pren.   She's just what I want and her I'll have.
 Li pas mandé robe moussiline,   A muslin gown she does n't choose,
 Li pas mandé déba brodé,   She does n't ask for broidered hose,
 Li pas mandé soulier prinelle,   She does n't want prunella shoes;
 C'est li mo oulé, c'est li ma pren.   O she's what I want and her I'll have.

The melody in the rhythm of a *Coonjai.* Melody and words of the second stanza from "Slave Songs of the United States," having been collected on the Good Hope plantation in St. Charles Parish in Louisiana. The arrangement was made by the author for George W. Cable's essay entitled "The Dance in the Place Congo," which appeared in the Century Magazine for February, 1886. Reprinted by permission of Mr. Cable and the Century Co.

Rémon, Rémon

Mo par-lé Ré-mon, Ré-mon, li par-lé Si-mon, Si-mon, li par-lé Ti-tine, Ti-tine, li tom-bé dans cha-grín. O femme Ro-mu-lus, Ohé! Belle femme Ro-mu-lus, O!— O femme Ro-mu-lus, O!— Belle femme, qui ça vou-lez mo fé.

A *Coonjai.* "I spoke to Rémon, he spoke to Simon, he spoke to Titine, who was stricken with grief. O, woman Romulus, beautiful woman Romulus, you have done to me what you wished." Words and melody from "Slave Songs of the United States." The arrangement by John Van Broekhoven, printed in the Century Magazine in George W. Cable's essay, "The Dance in Place Congo," is here reprinted by permission of Mr Cable and the Century Co.

in New Orleans in a letter to me dated January, 1885: "Yes, I have seen them dance, but they danced the Congo, and sang a purely African song to the accompaniment of a drygoods box beaten with a stick or bones and a drum made by stretching a skin over a flour barrel. As for the dance—in which the women do not take their feet off the ground—it is as lascivious as is possible. The men dance very differently, like savages leaping in the air."

To Mr. Hearn I owe several examples of Martinique folk-music, which were written down for him by a bandmaster in St. Pierre. (Page 126.) A fascinating combination of African and Spanish elements is found in the melody, which the collector called "Manmam Colette"—unquestionably a dance-song. On the bandmaster's transcription he had written directions that the first part (allegretto) be sung eight times; then comes the dance (allegro) ten times. The same directions probably applied also to "Ou beau di moin tête ou bien pomadée." The second part of the tune, to which the bandmaster gave the title "Dessan mouillage acheter daubanes," has a curious resemblance to a Tyrolean "yodel." It is probably the melody to which a ballad to which Hearn makes reference is sung:

Moin descenne Saint-Piè,
Acheté dobannes;
Auliè ces dobannes
C'est yon *bel bois* menmoin monté.

The spelling of the soft and musical creole patois is a matter of individual case, taste and fancy. The ballad tells the story of a youth of Fort de France who was sent to St. Pierre to buy a stock of earthenware water-jars (*dobannes*), but who fell in love with a colored girl and spent his father's money in buying her presents and a wedding outfit. Hearn cites the song to illustrate a pretty simile. The phrase "bel bois" is used to designate handsome people. "Toutt bel bois ka allé," said Manm-Robert, meaning that all the handsome people are passing away. "This is the very comparison made by Ulysses looking upon Nausicaa, though more naïvely expressed," comments our author.

Three Dance-tunes from Martinique
N⁰ 1. Manmam Colette

N⁰ 2. Ou beau di moin tête ou bien pomadée

N⁰ 3. Dessan mouillage acheter daubanes

Transcribed by a Bandmaster at St. Pierre and sent to the author by Lafcadio Hearn

[126]

CHAPTER X

SONGS OF THE BLACK CREOLES

THE LANGUAGE OF THE AFRO-AMERICAN FOLKSONGS—
PHONETIC CHANGES IN ENGLISH—GRAMMAR OF THE
CREOLE PATOIS—MAKING FRENCH COMPACT
AND MUSICAL—DR. MERCIER'S PAMPHLET—
CREOLE LOVE-SONGS

The circumstance that the folksongs of the slaves were preserved by oral tradition alone until nearly fifty years ago, when the first collection was printed, gives peculiar interest to a study of their language—or rather their languages, for the songs of the black creoles of Louisiana and the Antilles are also American folksongs, though they are sung in French patois and not in English. In both cases a fundamental phenomenon confronts us: The slave had to make the language in which he communicated with his master, or rather he had to reconstruct it orally without the help of written or printed books. Having made his patois, he forgot his own native tongue and perpetuated the new medium of communication in the same way in which he had learned and perpetuated the African language. After this had been done and the new tongue had become to him a vehicle for his rude artistic utterances, those utterances had to be retained by tradition and transmitted by word of mouth entirely. This brought with it a phenomenon with which students of ballads are familiar—the corruptions of texts due to the habit of accepting sound for sense. The slaves of the States in which the masters spoke English, under Protestant influences, heard the Biblical expressions which appealed powerfully to their imagination and emotions from their preachers, some of whom were as illiterate as the multitude they sought to enlighten. They heard their masters use many words of which they could only surmise the meaning, but which also appealed to them as resounding and mouth-filling. Like children they accepted the sounds without inquiring into the sense, or gave them meanings of their own. Such terms as "iggle-quarter," "count-aquils" and "ginny-bank" in the working song "Ho, round the corn, Sally," may be corruptions of French words heard from the Huguenot refugees. (Unless, indeed, "iggle-quarter" be eagle-quarter, "ginny-bank," the Bank of Virginia, and the lines have a financial sense.) Others have a more or less obvious interpretation. "Oh, my body rock 'long fever" may have well been carried away from a sickroom as the remark of master or mistress: "My body has long been racked by a fever." "Body racked wid pain" is a line in one of the songs which I have printed—"O'er the Crossing." I cannot accept the interpretation of "Daniel rock de lion joy" as "Daniel racked the lion's jaw," given in a footnote of "Slave Songs"; "locked the lion's jaw" is too obviously the correct reading. "An' de nineteen wile in his han'" is pretty plainly indicated as once having read: "The anointing oil in his hand" by the context, and "John sittin' on de golden order" was probably "John sitting on the golden altar"—a picture which could not fail to appeal to the fancy of the negroes, though I do not know where they found it.

The survival of words from African languages seems much smaller in the songs than in the folktales from Bahama which Professor Edwards prints in his book.[1] As I have intimated, these words would naturally be retained in songs connected with superstitious ceremonies and forbidden dances.

In his preface to "Slave Songs" Mr. Allen points out that "phonetic" decay had gone very far in the speech of the slaves, and with it "an extreme simplification of etymology and syntax." *Th* and *v* or *f* had been softened into *d* and *b*; *v* and *w* had been interchanged; words had been shorn of syllables which seemed redundant—as illustrated in "lee' bro' " for "little brother." The letters *n, v* and *r* were sometimes used euphonically, perhaps to gratify a melodic sense, as the vowel *a* frequently was for

[1] "Bahama Songs and Stories."

rhythmical effect. Mr. Allen gives an example of the euphonic *n*: "He de baddes' little gal from yere to *n*'Europe"; the interjection of *a*, as in "settin' side-a ob de holy Lamb," is very common.

There were contractions which scarcely call for comment, in view of what still happens every day among cultured white people in colloquial speech. The progress of "How do you do?" through "How d'ye do?" and "How dy'?" to "Huddy" is very patent, and we can scarcely deplore it in view of the singularly mellifluous and brisk line "Tell my Jesus huddy O." The grammatical simplifications were natural enough in a people who had to speak a language which they were not permitted to learn to read or write. *Em* was a pronoun which applied to all genders and both numbers; *been* and *done* as the past tenses of verbs are familiar to-day among other than the blacks in the South, as are many other peculiarities of grammar of which we cannot say whether the slaves borrowed them from the illiterate whites or the whites from them.

It is perhaps a little singular, though not impossible of explanation, that the negroes who came under the domination of the French colonists of Louisiana and the West Indies should have developed a patois or dialect, which is not only more euphonious than the language from which it was derived, but also have created a system of grammar which reflects credit upon their logical capacity and their musical instincts. The peculiarities of the English songs referred to are nearly all extinct, but the creole patois, though never reduced to writing for its users, is still a living language. It is the medium of communication between black nurses and their charges in the French families of Louisiana to-day, and half a century ago it was exclusively spoken by French creoles up to the age of ten or twelve years. In fact, children had to be weaned from it with bribes or punishment. It was, besides, the language which the slave spoke to his master and the master to him. The need which created it was the same as that which created the corrupt English of the slaves in other parts of the country. The Africans who were brought to America had no written language. Among them there was diversity of speech as well as of tribes and customs. The need of a medium of communication between them and their masters was greater than that of a communal language for themselves; and in its construction they had the help of their masters, who were not averse to a simplification of their colloquial speech. The African languages were soon forgotten. Dr. Alfred Mercier, who wrote a delightful brochure on the grammar of the creole patois some forty or more years ago,[1] says that there were then not more than six or seven African words in the language spoken by the creoles. His meaning, no doubt, was that only so many words were employed colloquially, for a great many more were in use in the incantations which formed a part of their superstitious rites and in some of the songs which accompanied their orgiastic dances, though their meaning was forgotten. How the black slave proceeded in the construction of a grammar for the speech which he took from the lips of his master is most interestingly described by Dr. Mercier in his pamphlet, on which I have drawn for the following notes:

In the first place, the negro composes the verb. For his present indicative he takes a pronoun and the adjective which qualifies a state of being. He says *Mo contan* (Je suis content) for "Moi être content"; he suppresses the infinitive (être). The present indicative tells us that the action expressed by the verb is doing. You present yourself at the door of a house and say to the negress who opens to your knock that you want to speak to her master. She replies that he dines (qu'il dîne); *i. e.*, he is dining (qu'il est dînant); to form the present participle she makes use of the pronoun *lui* (which she pronounces *li*) and places it before the preposition *après* (*apé*). Of these two words she makes one, *lapé*, to which she adds the infinitive dîner— *lapé dinin*—(il est après dîner).

The preposition *après* plays an important rôle in the creole patois. Dr. Mercier points out that it is used by the

[1] "Étude sur la Langue Créole en Louisiane," evidently printed for private circulation, and bearing neither imprint nor date.

negroes in the same sense in which it was employed long ago in France: *être après faire quelque chose,* to be after doing something—a locution found in Languedoc.[1] The creole negro takes the word indicating a state of being and prefixes the pronoun:

Mo—Je suis—I am
To—Tu es—Thou art } malade—ill.
Li—Il est—He is
Nou—Nous sommes—We are
Vou—Vous êtes—You are } malades—ill.
Ye—Ils sont—They are

To express an act in the course of accomplishment recourse is had to the pronoun joined to the preposition *après* (*apé*) which is followed by the infinitive: Moi après, *i. e.,* Mo apé, which is contracted into *mapé,* and so on with the rest:

Mapé
Tapé
Lapé } dinin.
Napé
Vapé
Yapé

the equivalent of

Je suis
Tu es
Il est } après dîner.
Nous sommes
Vous êtes
Ils sont

Nothing remains of the pronoun, except the sound of the initial letter, and these people having no written language, even the letter does not exist for them. When the black slave heard his master speak of things in the past tense it was the sound *té* which fell most frequently and persistently into his ear: J'étais, tu étais, il était, ils étaient. Upon this *té* the negro seized as representing or figuring the past, and joining it to the pronoun he formed his imperfect indicative of the verb être:

Moté—J'étais.
Toté—Tu étais.
Lité—Il était.
Nouté—Nous étions.
Vouté—Vous étiez.
Yeté—Ils étaient.

[1] I might add that it is a form with which the English language has been enriched by an Irish idiom.

The negro hears some one say to the white man who is expecting an arrival, "Il va venir." He recognizes that "va" as the sign of the future. For "Ce gros bateau à vapeur ne pourra pas descendre quand l'eau sera basse" he says: *Gro stimbotte-là pas capab decende can lo va basse.* To "va" he attached the infinitive of the verb to determine the kind of action, and the pronoun to indicate the actor. Thus *va chanté* tells us that there is to be singing. Who is to sing? The pronoun gives the information:

$$\left.\begin{array}{l} Mo \\ To \\ Li \\ Nou \\ Vou \\ Ye \end{array}\right\} va\ chanté.$$

This is the primitive stage of the process which in the mouth of the future creole undergoes two changes: The sound *va* is combined with the pronoun (*mova, tova, liva, nouva, vouva, yeva—chanté*), and then for economical contraction the sounds *ov, iv, ouv, ev* are elided, the initial letter of the pronoun is united with the radical sound *a*, and we have:

$$\left.\begin{array}{l} Ma \\ Ta \\ La \\ Na \\ Va \\ Ya \end{array}\right\} chanté.$$

Sometimes there is a still further contraction, the pronominal consonant disappearing, leaving the vowel *a* alone to represent the future. For the imperative mood the creole uses the infinitive, preceded by the noun or pronoun; for "Que Jules vienne avec vous" he says: *Jule vini ave vou.* The first person plural in the creole imperative is curious in that to form it he calls in the help of the imperative verb "aller," which he pronounces *anon;* "Traversons cette rue" becomes *anon traverse larue cila.* He escapes such embarrassments as "buvons," "dormons," "cousons" with the help of his ever-ready *anon—anon boi, anon dormi, anon coude.*

"In its transformation into creole," says Dr. Mercier, "French is simplified and acquires either grace or strength.

In many cases the verbs 'to be' (*être*) and 'to have' (*avoir*) disappear: *Li vaillan* (il est vaillant); *Li pas peur* (il n'a pas peur). In French the negative particles are over-abundant; it is one of the faults of the language. In the phrase 'Il n'a pas peur' there are two negatives, 'ne' and 'pas.' The creole uses only one and says in three words what the speaker of French says in five. The difference is still more apparent in the phrases "Je commence à être fatigué; je crois qu'il est temps de nous en retourner"— fourteen words; *Mo comance lasse; mo cré tan nou tournin* —eight. Moreover, fleetness is acquired by the suppression of the preposition 'à' and the conjunction 'que.' "

Obeying the law of laziness, or following the line of least resistance, the creole elides the letters which are difficult of pronunciation, or substitutes easy ones for them. The letter *r* is as difficult for the negro as it is for the Chinaman; he elides it and says *pou* for pour, *apé* for après, *di* for dire, *cate* for quatre. In Martinique, if I am to judge by my songs, when he does not dispense with the letter altogether he gives it a soft sound, like an infusion of *w* into *ou: ouôche* for roche. The French sound of *u* is as difficult for the negro as it is for the American or Englishman; he does not struggle with it, but substitutes the short sound of *i: torti* for tortue, *jige* for juge, or he uses the continental sound (oo): *la nouite* for la nuit, *tou souite* for tout de suite. *Eu* he changes to *ai*, as in air; *lonair* for l'honneur; *j* and *g* giving him trouble, he changes them to *z: touzou* for toujours, *zamais* for jamais, *manzé* for mangé. He has no use for the first person pronoun "je," *mo* sufficing him; and "tu" he replaces with *to* and *toi*. Words which are too long to suit his convenience he abbreviates at pleasure: *baracé*, embarrassé; *pelé*, appelé; *blié*, oublié.

Thus, then, grew the pretty language, soft in the mouth of the creole as *bella lingua in bocca toscana*, in which the creole sang of his love, gave rhythmical impulse to the dance, or scourged with satire those who fell under his displeasure—the uses to which the music was put which I purpose now to discuss. It should be borne in mind that the popular notion in the United States that a creole is a Louisiana negro is erroneous. Friedenthal discusses the origin of the word and its application in the introduction to his book "Musik, Tanz und Dichtung bei den Kreolen Amerikas." The Spanish word *criollo*, from which the French *créole* is derived, is a derivation from the verb *criar*, to create, bring up, breed. From this root other words are derived; not only substantives like *cria* (brood), *crianza* (education, bringing up), *criatura, criador*, etc., but also *criada* (servant), which in other languages has a very different etymology (*Diener, serviteur, domestique, servo*, etc.). The term *criado* is a relic of the old patriarchal system, under which the servants of the household were brought up by the family. Children of the servants became servants of the children of the master. So on the plantations of the Southern States slaves were set apart from childhood to be the playmates and attendants of the children of the family. *Criollo* also signifies things bred at home but born in foreign lands, and thus it came about that the Spaniard called his children born in foreign lands *criollos;* and as these foreign lands were chiefly the American colonies, the term came to be applied first to the white inhabitants of the French and Spanish colonies in America and only secondarily to the offspring of mixed marriages, regardless of their comparative whiteness or blackness.

When Lafcadio Hearn was looking up creole music for me in New Orleans in the early 80's of the last century, he wrote in one of his letters: "The creole songs which I have heard sung in the city are Frenchy in construction, but possess a few African characteristics of method. The darker the singer the more marked the oddities of intonation. Unfortunately, most of those I have heard were quadroons or mulattoes." In another letter he wrote: "There could neither have been creole patois nor creole melodies but for the French and Spanish blooded slaves of Louisiana and the Antilles. The melancholy, quavering beauty and weirdness of the negro chant are lightened by the French influence, or subdued and deepened by the Spanish." Hearn was musically illiterate, but his powers of observation were keen and his intuitions quick and penetrating. He felt what I have described as the imposition of French and Spanish melody on African rhythm. This union of elements is found blended with the French patois in the songs created by the creole negroes in Louisiana and the West Indies. Hearn came across an echo of the most famous of all creole love-songs in St. Pierre and in his fantastic manner gave it a habitation and a name. Describing the plague of smallpox in a chapter of "Two Years in the French West Indies," he tells of hearing a song coming up through the night, sung by a voice which had "that peculiar metallic timbre that reveals the young negress." Always it is one "melancholy chant":

> Pauv' ti Lélé,
> Pauv' ti Lélé!
> Li gagnin doulé, doulé, doulé,—
> Le gagnin doulé
> Tout pâtout!

I want to know who little Lélé was, and why she had pains "all over"—for however artless and childish these creole songs seem, they are invariably originated by some real incident. And at last somebody tells me that "poor little Lélé had the reputation of being the most unlucky girl in St. Pierre; whatever she tried to do resulted only in misfortune;—when it was morning she wished it were evening, that she might sleep and forget; but when the night came she could not sleep for thinking of the trouble she had had during the day, so that she wished it were morning. . . . "

Perhaps "Pov' piti Lolotte" (a portion of whose melody served Gottschalk, a New Orleans creole of pure blood, for one of his pianoforte pieces) came from the West Indies originally, but it is known throughout Creoleland now. It fell under the notice of Alphonse Daudet, who, Tiersot says, put it in the mouth of one of his characters in a novel. Out of several versions which I have collected I have put the song together, words and melody, in the form in which Mr. Burleigh has arranged it. (See page 136.) It is worth noting that the *coda* of the melody was found only in the transcript made from the singing of the slaves on the Good Hope plantation, in St. Charles Parish, La., and that this coda presents a striking use of the rhythmical snap which I have discussed in connection with the "spirituals," but which is not found in any one of them with so much emotional effect as here. In his essay in "The Cen-

Pov' piti Lolotte

lou po-té ma-drasse, li po-té ji-pon gar-ni. Ca-la-
quand po-té la chaîne, A-dieu cour-ri tout bon-heur, D'a-mour

lou po-té ma-drasse, li po-té ji-pon gar-ni.
quand po-té la chaîne, A-dieu cour-ri tout bon-heur.

Pov'piti Lolotte a mouin, Pov'pi-ti Lolotte a mouin, Li gagnin bo-bo, bo-bo, Li gagnin

dou-lé, dou-lé, dou-lé, Li gagnin dou-lé ___ dans ker à li.

Words and melody collated from various sources by the author. The arrangement made by
H. T. Burleigh.

tury Magazine" on creole songs Mr. Cable wrote:

One of the best of these creole love-songs . . . is the tender lament of one who sees the girl of his heart's choice the victim of chagrin in beholding a female rival wearing those vestments of extra quality that could only be the favors which both women had courted from the hand of some proud master whence alone such favors should come. "Calalou," says the song, "has an embroidered petticoat, and Lolotte, or Zizi," as it is often sung, "has a heartache." Calalou, here, I take to be a derisive nickname. Originally it is the term for a West Indian dish, a noted ragout. It must be intended to apply here to the quadroon women who swarmed into New Orleans in 1809 as refugees from Cuba, Guadaloupe and other islands where the war against Napoleon exposed them to Spanish and British aggression. It was with this great influx of persons, neither savage nor enlightened, neither white nor black, neither slave nor truly free, that the famous quadroon caste arose and flourished. If Calalou, in the verse, was one of these quadroon fair ones, the song is its own explanation.

In its way the song "Caroline" (see page 139) lets light into the tragedy as well as the romance of the domestic life of the young creole slaves. Marriage, the summit of a poor girl's ambition, is its subject—that state of blissful respectability denied to the multitude either by law or social conditions. I have taken words and melody from "Slave Songs," but M. Tiersot, who wrote the song down from the singing of a negress in New Orleans, gives the name of the heroine as Azélie and divides the poem into two stanzas separated by a refrain:

> Papa dit non, maman dit non,
> C'est li m'oulé, c'est li ma pren. (*Bis*)
> Un, deux, trois, Azélie.
> Pas paré com ça, ma chèr! (*Bis*)
>
> Sam'di l'amour, Dimanch' marié,
> Lundi matin piti dans bras;
> N'a pas couvert', n'a pas de draps,
> N'a pas a rien, piti dans bras!
>
> (Papa says no, mama says no.
> It is he whom I want and who will have me.
> One, two, three; don't talk that way, my dear!
> Saturday, love; Sunday, married;
> Monday morning, a little one in arms.
> There is no coverlet, no sheets, nothing—little one in arms!)

Tiersot gives the melody of the stanzas in 5-8 time, of the refrain in 2-4, and describes the movements of the dancers (the song is a Counjai) as a somewhat languorous turning with a slight swaying of the body. I have translated "cabanne" cabin, but in Martinique "caban" signifies a bed, and in view of M. Tiersot's variant text this may also have been the meaning of the term in Louisiana.

Caroline

Aine, dé, trois, Ca-ro-line, ça, ça, yé comme ça, ma chère!

Aine, dé, trois, Ca-ro-line, ça, ça, yé comme ça, ma chère!

Pa - pa di non, man-man di oui, C'est limo ou-lé, c'est li ma pren. Ya

pas lar-zan pou a-cheté cabanne, C'est limo ou-lé, c'est li ma pren.

Words and melody from "Slave Songs of the United States". The arrangement, by John Van Broekhoven, to a variant of the poem, was printed by Mr. Cable in his essay on "The Dance in Place Congo" and is here reprinted by permission of Mr. Cable and the Century Co., the words as sung on the Good Hope Plantation, St. Charles Parish, La., being restored. The meaning of the words is: "One, two, three, that's the way, my dear. Papa says no, mama says yes; 'Tis him I want and he that will have me. There will be no money to buy a cabin."

CHAPTER XI

SATIRICAL SONGS OF THE CREOLES

A Classification of Slave Songs—The Use of Music
in Satire—African Minstrels—The Carnival in
Martinique—West Indian Pillards—Old
Boscoyo's Song in New Orleans—Con-
clusion—An American School of
Composition

In an appendix to his "Bahama Songs and Stories"
Professor Edwards cites John Mason Brown as giving the
following classification of the songs of the slave in an
article printed in "Lippincott's Magazine" for Decem-
ber, 1868:

1. Religious songs, *e. g.*, "The Old Ship of Zion," where the refrain of
"Glory, halleloo" in the chorus keeps the congregation well together in the
singing and allows time for the leader to recall the next verse.

2. River songs, composed of single lines separated by a barbarous and
unmeaning chorus and sung by the deck hands and roustabouts mainly for
the howl.

3. Plantation songs, accompanying the mowers at harvest, in which the
strong emphasis of rhythm was more important than the words.

4. Songs of longing; dreamy, sad and plaintive airs describing the most
sorrowful pictures of slave life, sung in the dusk when returning home from
the day's work.

5. Songs of mirth, whose origin and meaning, in most cases forgotten,
were preserved for the jingle of rhyme and tune and sung with merry laughter
and with dancing in the evening by the cabin fireside.

6. Descriptive songs, sung in chanting style, with marked emphasis and
the prolongation of the concluding syllable of each line. One of these songs,
founded upon the incidents of a famous horse race, became almost an epidemic
among the negroes of the slave-holding States.

In this enumeration there is a significant omission. On
the plantations where Latin influences were dominant, in
New Orleans and the urban communities of the Antilles,
the satirical song was greatly in vogue. It might be said
that the use of song for purposes of satire cannot be said
to be peculiar to any one race or people or time; in fact,
Professor Henry T. Fowler, of Brown University, in his
"History of the Literature of Ancient Israel,"[1] intimates

[1] New York: The Macmillan Company, 1912, page 15.

that a parallel may exist between the "taunt songs" of primitive peoples, the Israelitish triumph songs, like that recorded in Numbers, xxi, 27-30, the Fescennine verses of the early Romans, and the satirical songs of the negroes of the West Indies. Nevertheless, there is scarcely a doubt in my mind but that the penchant for musical lampooning which is marked among the black creoles of the Antilles is more a survival of a primitive practice brought by their ancestors from Africa than a custom borrowed from their masters. What was borrowed was the occasion which gave the practice license.

This was the carnival, which fact explains the circumstance that the creole songs of satire are much more numerous in the French West Indies than in Louisiana. The songs are not only more numerous, but their performance is more public and more malicious in intent. The little song "Musieu Bainjo" (see page 142), melody and words of which came from a Louisiana plantation, though not wholly devoid of satrical sting, is chiefly a bit of pleasantry not calculated deeply to wound the sensibilities of its subject; very different are such songs as "Loéma tombé" (see page 147) and "Marie-Clémence" (see page 148), which Mr. Hearn sent me from Martinique. The verse-form, swinging melodic lilt and incisive rhythm of "Michié Préval" (see page 152) made it the most effective vehicle for satire which creole folksong has ever known, and Mr. Cable says that for generations the man of municipal politics was fortunate who escaped entirely a lampooning set to its air; but it is doubtful if even Mr. Préval, cordially hated as he was, had to endure such cruel and spectacular public castigation as the creators of the *pillard* still inflict on the victims of their hatred. These songs will come up for detailed consideration presently, but first it may be well to pursue the plan which I have followed in respect of the other elements of Afro-American folksong and point out the obvious African origin of this satirical element.

In many, perhaps in the majority of African tribes, there are professional minstrels whose social status now is curiously like that of the mountebanks, actors and secular

Musieu Bainjo

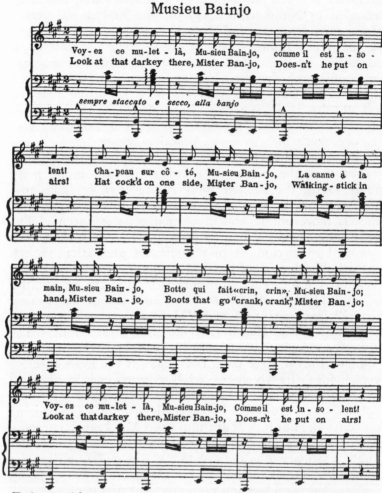

Words and melody of this song were noted on a plantation in St. Charles Parish, Louisiana, and first printed in "Slave Songs of the United States," the editor remarking that it is an "attempt of some enterprising negro to write a French song." The particularly propulsive effect of the African "snap" at the beginning is noteworthy. The translation, printed by Mr. Cable in the "Century Magazine", is used with his permission and that of the Century Co. In his comment on the song Mr. Cable remarks: "We have to lose the saucy double meaning between *mulet* (mule) and *mulâtre* (mulatto)." Arrangement by the author.

musicians in Europe a few centuries ago. That these black minstrels are not "beggars with one consent" is due to the fact that their powers of improvization are so great and their willingness to employ them to mercenary ends so well known that that they are feared as well as hated, and conciliated in the manner universal by those who can afford to do it. These men, who are called *Lashash* by the Soudanese, *Nzangah* (a term also applied to prostitutes) by the Niam-Niam, *griots*, or *guiriots*, in Senegambia and Guinea, and *guéhués* in West Africa, are sycophants attached to the bodies of kings and chiefs, for whom they exercise bardic functions. They are extremely sharp of tongue and have no hesitation in putting their skill to the basest of uses. Hence it comes that persons near enough to the sources of power and preferment approach them in the same manner in which suppliants for royal favor have approached the mistresses of kings and potentates in civilized countries time out of mind. Moreover, as their shafts are as much dreaded as their encomiums are desired, they collect as much tribute for what they withhold as for what they utter, and many of them grow rich. Thomas Ashley, in a book of travels published in 1745,[1] says that they are "reckoned rich, and their wives have more crystal blue stones and beads about them than the king's wives." But, like the mediæval European actors, jugglers and musicians, they are not recognized as reputable; they are even denied the rite of burial, and in some places their dead bodies are left to rot in hollow trees.

The weapon which these *griots* use against those whom they wish to injure is satire, and this species of poetical composition is a feature of the improvizations of the blacks in the Antilles to-day and long has been. Bryan Edwards says in his history of the English colonies in the West Indies:

Their songs are commonly *impromptu*, and there are among them individuals who resemble the *improvisatori*, or extempore bards of Italy; but I cannot say much for their poetry. Their tunes in general are characteristic of their national manners; those of the Eboes being soft and languishing; of the Koromantyus, heroick and martial. At the same time there is observable in most of them a predominant melancholy, which, to a man of feeling, is sometimes very affecting.

[1] Cited by Engel.

At their merry meetings and midnight festivals, they are not without ballads of another kind, adapted to such occasions, and here they give full scope to a talent for ridicule which is exercised not only against each other but also, not infrequently, at the expense of their owner or employer; but most part of their songs at these places are fraught with obscene ribaldry and accompanied with dances in the highest degree licentious and wanton.

That was in the eighteenth century, when vast numbers of the slaves were African by birth. At the end of the nineteenth century Hearn found that satire was still a prominent element in the songs of the black people of Martinique. He is speaking of the blanchisseuses, hard at work early in the morning in the rushing river at St. Pierre.

The air grows warmer; the sky blue takes fire; the great light makes joy for the washers; they shout to each other from distance to distance, jest, laugh, sing. Gusty of speech these women are; long habit of calling to one another through the roar of the torrent has given their voices a singular sonority and force; it is well worth while to hear them sing. One starts the song, the next one joins her; then another and another, till all the channel rings with the melody from the bridge of the Jardin des Plantes to the Pont-bois:

> "C'est, moin qui té, ka lavé,
> Passé, raccommodé;
> Y té néf hè disouè,
> Ou metté moin derhò,
> Yche moin assous bouas moin;
> Laplie té ka tombé—
> Léfan moin assous tête moin;
> Doudoux, ou m'abandonne;
> Moin pa ni pèsonne pou soigné moin."

("It was I who washed and ironed and mended; at 9 o'clock at night thou didst put me out of doors, with my child in my arms; the rain was falling, with my poor straw mattress upon my head! Doudoux! thou dost abandon me! . . . I have none to care for me."). . . . A melancholy chant— originally a carnival improvisation made to bring public shame upon the perpetrator of a cruel act; but it contains the story of many of these lives— the story of industrious, affectionate women temporarily united to brutal and worthless men in a country where legal marriages are rare. Half of the creole songs which I was able to collect during a residence of nearly two years in the island touch upon the same sad theme.

Of the carnival, at which these satirical songs spring up like poisonous fungi, Hearn draws a vivid picture, projecting it with terrible dramatic effect against an account of a plague of smallpox. There is a last masquerade before Lent, on Ash Wednesday—the carnival lasts a day longer in Martinique than anywhere else. Since January there has been dancing every day in the streets of St. Pierre; such dancing as might be indulged in, presumably, by decorous persons; but in the country districts African dances have been danced—such dances as the city never sees. Nevertheless, a cloud rests upon the gayety because *La Verette*, a terrible and unfamiliar visitor to the island, has made her advent. The pestilence, brought from Colón on the steamer in the preceding September, has now begun to sweep St. Pierre, as it had already swept Fort de France, as by a wind of death. Hundreds are dying, but there must be the usual procession of maskers, mummers and merry-makers. Three o'clock. There is a sound of drums. The people tumble into the streets and crowd into the public square:

> Simultaneously from north and south, from the Mouillage and the Fort, two immense bands enter the Grande Rue—the great dancing societies these—the *Sans-Souci* and the *Intrépides*. They are rivals; they are the composers and singers of those carnival songs—cruel satires most often, of which the local meaning is unintelligible to those unacquainted with the incident inspiring the improvisation, of which the words are too often coarse or obscene—whose burden will be caught up and re-echoed through all the burghs of the island. Vile as may be the motive, the satire, the malice, these chants are preserved for generations by the singular beauty of the airs, and the victim of a carnival song need never hope that his failing or his wrong will be forgotten; it will be sung long after he is in his grave.

All at once a hush comes over the mob; the drums stop and the maskers scatter. A priest in his vestments passes by, carrying the viaticum to some victim of the dreadful scourge. *"C'est Bon-Dié ka passe"*—"It is the Good-God who goes by." Then the merriment goes on. Night falls. The maskers crowd into the ballrooms, and through the black streets the Devil makes his last carnival round:

> By the gleam of the old-fashioned oil lamps hung across the thoroughfares I can make out a few details of his costume. He is clad in red, wears a hideous blood-colored mask and a cap on which the four sides are formed by four looking-glasses, the whole headdress being surmounted by a red lantern. He has a white wig made of horsehair to make him look weird and old—since the Devil *is* older than the world. Down the street he comes, leaping nearly his own height, chanting words without human significance and followed by some three hundred boys, who form the chorus to his chant, all clapping hands together and giving tongue with a simultaneity that testifies how strongly the sense of rhythm enters into the natural musical feeling of the African—a feeling powerful enough to impose itself upon all Spanish-America and there create the unmistakable characteristics of all that is called "creole music."

> > *"Bimbolo!"*
> > *"Zimabolo!"*
> > *"Bimbolo!"*
> > *"Zimabolo!"*
> > *"Et Zimbolo!"*
> > *"Et bolo-po!"*

sing the Devil and his chorus. His chant is cavernous, abysmal—booms from his chest like the sound beaten in the bottom of a well. . . *"Ti manmaille-la, baill moin lavoix!"* ("Give me voice, little folk, give me voice.") And all chant after him in a chanting like the rushing of many waters and with triple clapping of hands: *"Ti manmaille-la baill moin lavoix!".* . . Then he halts before a dwelling in the Rue Peysette and thunders:
"Eh! Marie-sans-dent! Mi! diabe-la derho!"

That is evidently a piece of spite work; there is somebody living there against whom he has a grudge. . .
"Hey! Marie-without-teeth! Look! The Devil is outside!"
And the chorus catch the clew.
Devil: *"Eh! Marie-sans-dent!"*
Chorus: *"Marie-sans-dent! Mi! diabe-la derho!"*
Devil: *"Eh! Marie-sans-dent!"*
Chorus: *"Marie-sans-dent! Mi! diabe-la derho!"*
Devil *"Eh! Marie-sans-dent!"* etc.

The Devil at last descends to the main street, always singing the same song. I follow the chorus to the Savanna, where the route makes for the new bridge over the Roxelane, to mount the high streets of the old quarter of the Fort, and the chant changes as they cross over:

Devil: *"Oti oue diabe-la passe larivie?"* ("Where did you see the Devil going over the river?") And all the boys repeat the words, falling into another rhythm with perfect regularity and ease: *"Oti oue diabe-la passe larivie?"*

. . . .
. . . .
February 22d.
Old physicians indeed predicted it, but who believed them?

. . . .
. . . .
February 23d.
A coffin passes, balanced on the heads of black men. It holds the body of Pascaline Z., covered with quicklime.

It is thus that the satirical songs are made in Martinique, thus that they are disseminated. Latin civilization is less cruel to primitive social institutions than Anglo-Saxon— less repressive and many times more receptive. Sometimes it takes away little and gives much, as it has done with African music transplanted to its new environment. It has lent the charm of graceful melody to help make the sting of creole satire the sharper; but through the white veneer the black savagery sometimes comes crashing to proclaim its mastery in servitude. So in the case of the song "Loéma tombé"; so also in "Marie-Clémence." (See p. 148.) The latter is a carnival song which, if Hearn was correctly informed, was only four years old when he sent it to me. It is a fine illustration of that sententious dramaticism which is characteristic of folk-balladry the world over— that quick, direct, unprepared appeal to the imaginative

[146]

Loéma tombé

A *pillard* (satirical song) from Martinique, collected for the author in 1887 by Lafcadio Hearn and published by him in the appendix to his book "Two Years in the French West Indies" (Harper & Bros., 1890). Arrangement by Frank van der Stucken. Reprinted by permission of Harper & Bros.— In sending the song to the author Mr. Hearn wrote: "'Loéma tombé' is a *pillard*, a satirical chorus chanted with clapping of hands. Loéma was a girl who lived near the Pont-Bas and affected virtue. It was learned that she received not one but many lovers. Then the women came and sang:

(Solo) You little children there
Who live by the riverside,
You tell me truly this:
Did you see Loéma fall?
(Cho.) Tell me truly this: Loéma fall *(ad lib.)*"

Marie-Clémence

Words and melody from Lafcadio Hearn's "Two Years in the French West Indies," for which work they were arranged by this author. They were written down by a bandmaster in Martinique. In transmitting them to Mr. Krehbiel Mr. Hearn wrote: "'Marie-Clémence is a carnival satire composed not more than four years ago. The song was sung to torment Marie-Clémence, who was a vender of cheap cooked food." The exclamation 'Aïe!' is an example of the yell which occurs frequently in African music. The words mean: "Marie-Clémence is cursed; cursed, too, is her fried salt codfish *(lamori fritt)*, her gold bead necklace *(collier-choux)*, all her load." Now Marie speaks: "Aïe! Let me be, or I shall drown myself behind yon pile of rocks!" The song is reprinted by permission of Harper & Bros.

comprehension of a people whose life is fully expressed in the song of its own creation. Marie-Clémence was a *Machanne lapacotte*, a vendor of cooked food; chiefly, it would seem from the text, of salt codfish (*lamori fritt*). Why she should have been made the victim of popular hatred I do not know—perhaps never shall know, now that the ashes of La Pelée have made a winding-sheet for St. Pierre; but one day the devil pointed his finger at the poor woman and pronounced her codfish accursed, also her gold-bead necklace (*collier-choux*) and everything that she carried in the wooden bowl above her gay *madrasse*. An agony of pain and rage bursts out in the African exclamation "Aïe!" only to give way to her pitiful plaint:

> *Lagué moin, lagué moin, lagué moin!*
> *Moin ké néyé co main,*
> *Enbas gouôs pile ouôche-la!*

("Let me be, let me be, let me be! I shall drown myself behind yon pile of rocks!")

Sometimes the people of the Antilles do not wait for the coming of the carnival and its devil to punish those who have fallen under their displeasure. The custom of the *pillard* prevails in Martinique and can be practised at any time. Hearn writes: "Some person whom it is deemed justifiable or safe to annoy may suddenly find himself followed in the street by a singing chorus of several hundred, all clapping their hands and dancing or running in perfect time, so that all the bare feet strike the ground together. Or, the *pillard* chorus may even take up its position before the residence of the party disliked and then proceed with its performances." The song "Loéma tombé" (see page 147) provides an illustration. "Loéma," wrote Mr. Hearn, in sending me the words and melody of the song, "was a girl who lived near the Pont-Bas and affected virtue. It was learned that she received not one but many lovers. Then the women came and sang:

> *Solo:* You little children there
> Who live by the riverside,
> Tell me truly this:
> Did you see Loéma fall?
>
> *Chorus:* Tell me truly this: Loéma fall, etc.

SATIRICAL SONGS OF THE CREOLES

Local tradition in New Orleans may have preserved the date of the incident which gave rise to what in one of my notes I find called "Old Boscoyo's Song" (see page 152), but it has not got into my records. Mr. Cable calls the victim of the satire "a certain Judge Préval," and old residents of New Orleans have told me that he was a magistrate. If so, it would seem that he not only gave a ball which turned out to be a very disorderly affair, but also violated a law by giving it without a license. Many of the dancers found their way into the calaboose, and he had to pay a fine for his transgression and live in popular contumely ever afterward. From various sources I have pieced together part of the song in the original, and in the translation have included several stanzas for which at present I have only the English version in an old letter written by Hearn:

> Michié Préval li donnin gran bal,
> Li fé neg' payé pou sauter in pé.
>
> Dans l'écui vié la yavé gran gala,
> Mo cré soual la yé té bien étonné.
>
> Michié Préval li té Capitaine bal,
> Et so coché, Louis té maitr' cérémonie.
>
> Y'avé dé négresse belles passé maitresse,
> Qui volé belbel dans l'ormoire momselle.
>
> "Comment, Sazou, té volé mo cuilotte?"
> "Non, no maitr', mo di vous mo zes prend bottes."
>
> Ala maitr' geole li trouvé si drole,
> Li dit: "Moin aussi mo fé bal ici."
>
> Yé prend maitr' Préval yé metté li prison,
> Pasque li donnin bal pou volé nous l'arzan.

Monsieur Préval gave a big ball; he made the darkies pay for their little hop.
The grand gala took place in the stable; I fancy the horses were greatly amazed.
M. Préval was Captain of the ball; his coachman, Louis, was Master of Ceremonies.
(He gave a supper to regale the darkies; his old music was enough to give one the colic!)
(Then the old Jackass came in to dance; danced precisely as he reared, on his hind legs.)
There were negresses there prettier than their mistresses; they had stolen all manner of fine things from the wardrobes of their young mistresses.
(Black and white both danced the bamboula; never again will you see such a fine time.)
(Nancy Latiche (?) to fill out her stockings put in the false calves of her madame.)
"How, now, Sazou, you stole my trousers?" "No, my master, I took only your boots."
(And a little Miss cried out: "See here, you negress, you stole my dress.")

Michié Préval

A satirical song. Words (one stanza only) from Mr. Macrum's collection, by permission of the Century Co.; melody written down by the author at one of Mr. Cable's readings; arrangement by Mr. John VanBroekhoven.

It all seemed very droll to the keeper of the jail; he said, "I'll get up a dance (of another sort) for you here."

(At Mr. Préval's, in Hospital street, the darkies had to pay for their little hop.)

He took M. Préval and put him in the lock-up, because he gave a ball to steal our money.

(Poor M. Préval! I guess he feels pretty sick; he'll give no more balls in Hospital street.)

(He had to pay $100 and had a pretty time finding the money.)

(He said: "Here's an end of that; no more balls without a permit.")

In conclusion, a word on the value of these Afro-American folksongs as artistic material and their possible contribution to a national American school of music. In a large sense the value of a musical theme is wholly independent of its origin. But for a century past national schools have been founded on folksongs, and it is more than likely, in spite of the present tendency toward "impressionism" and other æsthetic aberrations, that composers will continue to seek inspiration at its source. The songs which I have attempted to study are not only American because they are products of a people who have long been an integral part of the population of America, but also because they speak an idiom which, no matter what its origin, Americans have instinctively liked from the beginning and have never liked more than now. On this point Dr. Dvořák, one of the world's greatest nationalists, is entitled to speak with authority. In an essay on "Music in America," which was printed in "The Century Magazine" for February, 1895, he said:

"A while ago I suggested that inspiration for truly national music might be derived from the negro melodies or Indian chants. I was led to take this view partly by the fact that the so-called plantation songs are indeed the most striking and appealing melodies that have been found on this side of the water, but largely by observation that this seems to be recognized, though often unconsciously, by most Americans. All races have their distinctive national songs, which they at once recognize as their own even if they have never heard them before. . . It is a proper question to ask, What songs, then, belong to the American and appeal more strikingly to him than any others? What melody would stop him on the street if he were in a strange land, and make the home feeling well up within him, no matter how hardened he might be, or how wretchedly the tune were played? Their number, to be sure, seems to be limited. The most potent, as well as the most beautiful among them, according to my estimation, are certain of the so-called plantation melodies and slave songs, all of which are distinguished by unusual and subtle harmonies, the thing which I have found in no other songs but those of Scotland and Ireland."

[153]

Dr. Dvořák's contention that material for music in the highest artistic forms might be found in the songs of the American negroes, which was derided by quite a number of American musicians, was long ago present in the appreciative and discriminating mind of Mrs. Kemble, who, in her life on a Georgian plantation, wished that some great composer might hear the "semi-savage" performances of the slaves, and said: "With a very little skilful adaptation and instrumentation I think one or two barbaric chants and choruses might be evoked from them that would make the fortunes of an opera." The opera is not yet forthcoming, but Dr. Dvořák's "From the New World," which drew its inspiration from Afro-American songs, is the most popular of his symphonies, and his American quartet has figured on the programmes of the Kneisel Quartet oftener than any other work in its repertory.

In the sense which seems to be playing hide and seek in the minds of the critics and musicians who object to the American label, there is no American music and can be none: Every element of our population must have its own characteristic musical expression, and no one element can set up to be more American than another. But suppose the time come when the work of amalgamation shall be complete and the fully evolved American people have developed a fondness for certain peculiarities of melody and rhythm, which fondness in turn shall disclose itself in a decided predilection for compositions in which those peculiarities have been utilized; will that music be American? Will it be racy of the soil? Will such compositions be better entitled to be called American than the music of Dr. Dvořák, which employs the same elements, but confesses that it borrows them from the songs of the Southern negroes? The songs are folksongs in the truest sense; that is, they are the songs of a folk, created by a folk, giving voice to the emotional life of a folk; for which life America is responsible. They are beautiful songs, and Dr. Dvořák has shown that they can furnish the inspiration for symphonic material to the composer who knows how to employ it. To use this material most effectively it is necessary to catch something of the spirit of the people to whom it is, or at least it seems, idiomatic. A native-born American ought to be able to do this quicker and better than a foreigner, but he will not be able to do it at all unless he have the gift of transmuting whatever he sees or feels into music; if he have it not, he will not write music at all; he might as well be a Hottentot as an American.

Though it has been charged against me, by intimation at least, it has never occurred to me in the articles which I have written on the subject to claim that with his symphony Dr. Dvořák founded a national school of composition. The only thing that I have urged in the matter is, that he has shown that there are the same possibilities latent in the folksongs which have grown up in America as in the folksongs of other peoples. These folksongs are accomplished facts. They will not be added to, for the reason that their creators have outgrown the conditions which alone made them possible. It is inconceivable that America shall add to her store of folksongs. Whatever characteristics of scales or rhythm the possible future American school of composition is to have must, therefore, be derived from the songs which are now existent. Only a small fraction of these songs have been written down, and to those which have been preserved the scientific method has not yet fully been applied. My effort, as I have confessed, is tentative. It ought to be looked upon as a privilege, if not a duty, to save them, and the best equipped man in the world to do this, and afterward to utilize the material in the manner suggested by Dr. Dvořák, ought to be the American composer. Musicians have never been so conscious as now of the value of folksong elements. Music is seeking new vehicles of expression, and is seeking them where they are most sure to be found—in the field of the folksong. We have such a field; it is rich, and should be cultivated.

APPENDIX

Weeping Mary

If there's an-y-bod-y here like {weep-ing_ Ma-ry, / pray-ing_ Sam-uel, / doubt-ing_ Thom-as,} Call up-on your Je-sus, and He'll draw nigh. O,— glo-ry, glo-ry hal-le-lu-jah! Glo-ry be to my God, who rules on high!

A "spiritual" from Boyle Co., Kentucky, noted by Miss Mildred J. Hill, of Louisville; harmonization by Henry Holden Huss, of New York. A striking example of the major sixth in a minor melody.

Some Come Cripple

A "shout" song from Boyle Co., Kentucky, collected for the author by Miss Mildred J. Hill, of Louisville. Arranged for this publication by Arthur Mees. The old woman, an ex-slave, who sang it for Miss Hill had forgotten the second line of the first stanza, and repeated the first as indicated.

Neve' a Man speak like this Man
("O! look-a death")

Words and melody from "Bahama Songs and Stories," by Charles L. Edwards, Ph. D., published for the American Folk-Lore Society by Houghton, Mifflin & Co., Boston, and reprinted by permission. The arrangement by H. T. Burleigh.
"Then came the officers to the chief priests and Pharisees; and they said unto them, Why
have ye not brought him? The officers answered, Never man spake like this man." St. John
vii: 45-46.

Jesus Heal' de Sick

Words and melody from "Bahama Songs and Stories", by Charles L. Edwards, Ph.D., published
for the American Folk-Lore Society by Houghton, Mifflin & Co. and reprinted by permission.
The arrangement made for this work by H. T. Burleigh.

Opon de Rock

Op-on de rock, op-on de rock, op-on de rock let de wa-ter run out. Op-on de rock, op-on de rock, op-on de rock of a - ges.

Words and melody from "Bahama Songs and Stories," by Charles L. Edwards, Ph.D., published for the American Folk-Lore Society by Houghton, Mifflin & Co. and reprinted by permission. The arrangement made for this work by H. T. Burleigh.

Nobody Knows the Trouble I See

Arranged for men's voices by Arthur Mees for the Mendelssohn Glee Club of New York. Printed here by permission.

Roll, Jordan, Roll

* "Parson Fuller," "Deacon Henshaw," "Brudder Mosey," "Massa Linkum," – etc.

2. Little chil'en, learn to fear de Lord, | 3. O, let no false nor spiteful word
   And let your days be long; | Be found upon your tongue;
   Roll, Jordan, etc. | Roll, Jordan, etc.

Words and melody from "Slave Songs of the United States." Arranged for men's voices by
Arthur Mees for the Mendelssohn Glee Club of New York, and published here by permission.
It is an interesting example of the use of the flat seventh

[165]

Ma mourri

oui, 'no - cent, ma mour - ri. Mo con-nin, zins zens, ma mour - ri,
yes, cra - zy, I must die. Well I know, young men, I must die,

oui, 'no - cent, ma mour - ri. Mo con - nin, zins zens,
yes, cra - zy, I must die. Well I know, young men,

ma mour - ri 'no - cent, ma mour - ri pou' la belle La - yotte!
I must, cra - zy, die, I must die for the fair La - yotte!

Words and music from the "Century Magazine" of February, 1886, where credit for the arrangement was inadvertently given to the author; it belongs to John VanBroekhoven. The translation is Mr. Cable's.

Martinique Love-Song

To, to, to!	Tap, tap, tap!
Ça qui là?	Who taps there?
C'est moin-menme l'anmou,	'Tis my own self, love,
Ouvé la pote ba moin.	Open the door for me.
To, to, to!	Tap, tap, tap!
Ça qui là?	Who taps there?
C'est moin-menme l'anmou,	'Tis my own self, love,
La plie ka mouillé moin.	The rain is wetting me.
To, to, to!	Tap, tap, tap!
Ça qui là?	Who taps there?
C'est moin-menme l'anmou,	'Tis my own self, love,
Qui ka ba on rhè moin!	Who give my heart to thee!

Collected for the author by Lafcadio Hearn, who says of it in his "Two Years in the French West Indies": "'To, to, to' is very old – dates back, perhaps, to the time of the *belles-affranchies*. It is seldom sung now except by survivors of the old régime: the sincerity and tenderness of the emotion that inspired it – the old sweetness of heart and simplicity of thought – are passing for ever away." The arrangement was made by Frank van der Stucken and is here reprinted by permission of Harper & Bros.

Emgann Sant-Kast
(The Battle of St. Cast)

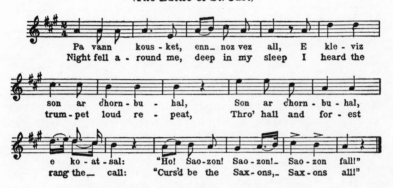

Pa vann kous-ket, enn_ noz vez all, E kle_ viz
Night fell a - round me, deep in my sleep I heard the

son ar c'horn-bu-hal, Son ar c'horn-bu-hal,
trum-pet loud re-peat, Thro' hall and for-est

e ko-at-sal: "Ho! Sao-zon! Sao-zon!_ Sao-zon fall!"
rang the_ call: "Curs'd be the Sax-ons,_ Sax-ons all!"

Rhyvelgyrch Cadpen Morgan
(Captain Morgan's March)

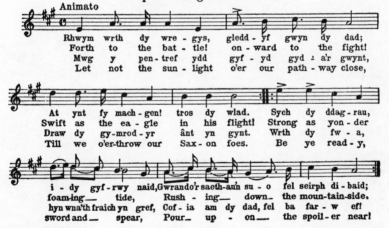

Animato

Rhwym wrth dy wre-gys, gledd-yf gwyn dy dad;
Forth to the bat-tle! on-ward to the fight!
Mwg y pen-tref ydd gyf-yd gyd ·a'r gwynt,
Let not the sun-light o'er our path-way close,

At ynt fy mach-gen! tros dy wlad. Sych dy ddag-rau,
Swift as the ea-gle in his flight! Strong as yon-der
Draw dy gy-mrod-yr ânt yn gynt. Wrth dy fw-a,
Till we o'er-throw our Sax-on foes. Be ye read-y,

i-dy gyf-rwy naid, Gwrando'r saeth-aun su-o fel seirph di-baid;
foam-ing_ tide, Rush-ing_ down_ the moun-tain-side.
hyn wna'th fraich yn gref, Cof-ia am dy dad, fel ba far-w ef!
sword and_ spear, Pour_ up-on_ the spoil-er near!

INDEX

Acadian Boat-Song, 51, 54.
Adelelmo, 59.
African travellers, musically illiterate, 13; idioms in American folksongs, 22; music, 56 *et seq.;* music characterized, 60; recitative in, 100; languages, survival of words from, 128.
Agwas, 57.
Aïda, Oriental melodies from, 87.
Ain't I glad I got out of the Wilderness, 15.
Albertini, 59.
Alla zoppa, 94.
Allen, William Francis, vi, 29, 32, 34, 43, 81, 97, 111, 129.
American Folk-Lore Society, viii; Indian music, 51.
Americans, what are they?, 26.
And I yearde from heaven to-day, 103.
Aridas, 57.
Ashantee music, 61.
Ashley, Thomas, quoted, 143.
Asra, Der, song by Rubinstein, 87.
Atlantic Monthly, quoted, 43.
Aurore Pradère, 123.
Awassas, 57.

Babouille, dance, 116.
Bach, Sonata in E, 15.
Bacon, Theodore, "Some Breton Folksongs," 9.
Balatpi, songs of the, 101.
Balboa, his ships built by negroes, 26.
Ballets, 16.
Baltimore Gals, 15.
Bamboula, dance, 116.
Barzaz-Breiz, 9.
Battle-Cry of Freedom, 17, 23.
Bechuanas, 60.
Bede, the Venerable, 36.
Beethoven, use of the major sixth in minor, 81.
Bélé, dance, 66, 116.
Bell da Ring, 49.
Benguin, dance, 116.
Bescherelle, quoted, 116.
Biblical allusions in songs, 45.
Blanchisseuses of St. Pierre, their songs, 144.
Bongo negroes, songs and dances of, 44, 113.
Bornou, song in praise of the Sultan of, 102.
Bouéné, dance, 116.
Bowditch, "Mission from Cape Coast Castle to Ashantee," 60, 62.
Brittany, folksongs of, 9.
Bryant's Minstrels, 33.

Buchner, Max, "Kamerun," quoted, 67.
Buffalo Gals, 15.
Bulgarians, folksongs of the, 7.
Burial customs of the Africans and slaves, 103 *et seq.*
Burleigh, Henry T., his help acknowledged, viii.
Burney, Dr. Charles, quoted, 72.
Burtchell, W. T., "Travels in the Interior of Africa," quoted, 60.
Burton, Richard F., "Lake Regions of Central Africa," quoted, 44, 57, 101.
Busch, Moritz, "Wanderungen zwischen Hudson und Mississippi," quoted, 12

Cable, George W., credited and quoted, viii, 38, 40, 138, 141.
Calhoun School Collection of Plantation Songs, quoted, 43, 71, 82, 87.
Calinda (*and* Caleinda), a dance, 66, 67, 116.
Cameron, Verney Lovett, "Across Africa," quoted, 101, 113.
Camptown Races, 16.
Canada, folksongs of, vi, 22.
Can't stay behind, 49.
Capello and Ivens, "From Benguela to the Territory of Yucca,"quoted, 113.
Captain Morgan's March, 10, 169.
Carnival celebration and songs in Louisiana and the French West Indies, 141 *et seq.*
Caroline, 138, 139.
Cassuto, 121.
Cata (*or* Chata), a dance, 116.
Century Company and Magazine, credited and quoted, viii, 30, 38, 40, 138, 152.
Chadwick, George W., writes American music, v.
Charleston Gals, 15.
China, use of pentatonic scale in its music, 7; a missionary's experience with hymns, 76.
Christy's Minstrels, 12, 15.
Classification of Slave Songs, 140.
Coleridge-Taylor, Samuel, composer, 44, 47, 59, 73.
Collections of Slave Songs, 42, 43.
Columbus, negroes come with him to America, 26.
Combat de Saint-Cast, 9, 169.
Come trembl-ing down, 84, 85, 87.
Congo, a dance, 126.
Congos, their music, 57.

052083